Home Rule Charters of California

Volume 3: Buena Park, Burbank, Carlsbad, Cerritos, and Chico

Bootblack Budget Books

Copyright 2020 ©

ISBN: 9798647581044

Disclaimer:

This book is for entertainment and educational purposes only. This book in no way represents legal advice of any type. This book also does not represent an official copy or publication of any government body. Readers are encouraged to contact their local municipality for official copies of home rule charters.

Table of Contents

The Home Rule Charter of
The City of Buena Park, California   **Page 4**

The Home Rule Charter of
The City of Burbank, California   **Page 11**

The Home Rule Charter of
The City of Carlsbad, California   **Page 59**

The Home Rule Charter of
The City of Cerritos, California   **Page 73**

The Home Rule Charter of
The City of Chico, California   **Page 118**

**The Home Rule Charter of
The City of Buena Park, California**

Table of Contents

Preamble **Page 6**

Article I: **Municipal Affairs Generally** **Page 7**

Section 100: Municipal Affairs; Generally

Article II: **General Laws** **Page 8**

Section 100: General Law Powers

Article III: **Public Contracting** **Page 9**

Section 100: Public Contracting

Article IV: **Interpretation** **Page 10**

Section 100: Construction and Interpretation

Section 200: Severability

Preamble

We the people of the City of Buena Park declare our intent to restore to our community the historic principles of self governance inherent in the doctrine of home rule. Sincerely committed to the belief that local government has the closest affinity to the people governed, and firm in the conviction that the economic and fiscal independence of our local government will promote the health safety and welfare of all the citizens of this City, we do hereby exercise the express right granted by the Constitution of the State of California to enact and adopt this Charter for the City of Buena Park.

Article I: Municipal Affairs Generally

Section 100: Municipal Affairs; Generally

The City shall have full power and authority to adopt make exercise and enforce ail legislation laws and regulations, and to take all actions relating to municipal affairs without limitation, which may be lawfully adopted made exercised taken or enforced under the Constitution of the State of California.

Article II: General Laws

Section 100: General Law Powers

In addition to the power and authority granted by the terms of this Charter and the Constitution of the State of California, the City shall have the power and authority to adopt, make exercise, and enforce all legislation laws and regulations, and to take all actions and to exercise any and all rights, powers, and privileges heretofore or hereafter established, granted, or prescribed by any law of the State of California, or by any other lawful authority. In the event of any conflict between the provisions of this Charter and the provisions of the general laws of the State of California, the provisions of this Charter shall control.

Article III: Public Contracting

Section 100: **Public Contracting**

The provisions of California Labor Code Section 1770 et. Seq. regarding prevailing wages on public works and related regulations, as now existing and as may be amended, are accepted and made applicable to the City, its departments, boards, officers, agents, and employees.

Article IV: Interpretation

Section 100: **Construction and Interpretation**

The language contained in this Charter is intended to be permissive rather than exclusive or limiting and shall be liberally and broadly construed in favor of the exercise by the City of ifs power to govern with respect to any matter which is a municipal affair.

Section 200: **Severability**

If any provision of this Charter should beheld by a court of competent jurisdiction to be invalid, void, or otherwise unenforceable, the remaining provisions shall remain enforceable to the fullest extent permitted by law

The electors of the City of Buena Park, by a majority of the votes cast, adopted this Charter of the City of Buena Park at the general municipal election held November 4 2008. The results of such election were certified by the City Council of the City of Buena Park through adoption of its Resolution No 12164

James A. Dow, Mayor

Certified and Attested By

Attest:

Shalice Reynoso, City Clerk

**The Home Rule Charter of
The City of Burbank, California**

Table of Contents

Preamble **Page 17**

Article 1:	**Name, Seal and Boundaries**	**Page 18**

Section 100: Name

Section 105: Seal

Section 110: Boundaries

Article 2:	**Powers**	**Page 19**

Section 200: Powers

Section 205: Joint Powers

Section 210: Administering Oaths and Subpoenas

Section 215: General Laws and Procedures

Article 3:	**Officers and Employees**	**Page 21**

Section 300: Officers and Employees

Section 305: The City Council

Section 310: Mayor

Section 315: City Manager

Section 320: City Attorney

Section 325: City Clerk

Section 330:	City Treasurer
Section 332:	City Tax Collector
Section 335:	Chief of Police
Section 340:	Fire Chief
Section 370:	Official Bonds
Section 375:	Oath of Office
Section 380:	Additional Duties of Officers
Section 385:	Compensation
Section 390:	Employees' Retirement System
Section 395:	Civil Service System
Article 4:	**Meetings of the Council** **Page 31**
Section 400:	Meetings, Regular and Special
Section 405:	Public Participation
Section 410:	Quorum
Article 5:	**Council Actions and Enactments** **Page 33**
Section 500:	Ordinances, Resolutions or Motions
Section 505:	Adoption of Codes by Reference

Article 6:	**City Departments and Governmental Functions**	**Page 35**

Section 600:   Governmental Functions

Section 605:   Department Structure

Section 610:   Utility Department

Article 7:	**Boards, Commissions and Committees**	**Page 37**

Section 700:   Boards, Commissions & Committees

Section 705:   Police Commission

Article 8:	**Elections**	**Page 39**

Section 800:   Elections

Section 805:   Canvass of Returns

Section 810:   Qualification for Elective Office

Section 815:   Initiative, Referendum and Recall

Article 9:	**Vacancies**	**Page 46**

Section 900:   Vacancies

Article 10:	**Finances and Budget**	**Page 47**

Section 1000:   Fiscal Year

Section 1005:   Budget

Section 1010:   Municipal Bonded Indebtedness

Section 1015:	Deposits with Treasurer	
Section 1020:	Payment of City Funds	
Section 1025:	Surplus Bond Money	
Section 1030:	Uniform Accounts and Reports	
Section 1035:	Independent Auditor	
Section 1040:	Financial Reports	
Section 1045:	Approving Illegal Claims	
Article 11:	**Board of Education**	**Page 52**
Section 1100:	Board of Education	
Article 12:	**Purchasing, Contracts, Franchises, Improvements and Property**	**Page 53**
Section 1200:	Public Improvements & Street Work	
Section 1205:	Contract Work and Purchases	
Section 1210:	Illegal and Void Contracts	
Section 1215:	Franchises	
Section 1220:	Disposition of Real Property	

Article 13:	**Official Records and Official Notices**	**Page 56**
Section 1300:	Official Records	
Section 1305:	Newspaper Advertising	
Article 14:	**Amendments**	**Page 57**
Section 1400:	Charter Amendments	
Article 15:	**Continuation of Previous Ordinances and Contracts; Constitutionality**	**Page 58**
Section 1500:	Continuing Ordinances In Force	
Section 1505:	Continuing Contracts In Force	
Section 1510:	Constitutional Clause	

Preamble

We, the people of the City of Burbank, in order to exercise the benefits of home rule and establish a responsive, effective and accountable government that maintains the highest level of integrity, provides an outstanding quality of life through excellent municipal services, and through which all voices in our diverse society can be heard, and to provide fair representation and distribution of government resources and a safe, harmonious, and sustainable environment based on principles of liberty and equality, do enact this Charter.

Article 1: Name, Seal and Boundaries

Section 100: Name

The municipal corporation now existing and known as "The City of Burbank" shall remain and continue as at present, in fact and in law, by the name of the "City of Burbank", and by such name shall have perpetual succession.

Section 105: Seal

The Council may by ordinance adopt a seal for the City.

Section 110: Boundaries

The boundaries of the City of Burbank shall continue as now established until changed as authorized by law.

Article 2: Powers

Section 200: **Powers**

The City of Burbank, by and through its Council and other officials, boards, commissions, committees and employees, shall have and may exercise all powers necessary or appropriate to a municipal corporation and the general welfare of its inhabitants, which are not prohibited by the California Constitution and this Charter, and which it would be competent for this Charter to set forth particularly or specifically; and the specification in this Charter of any particular powers shall not be held to be exclusive or any limitation upon this general grant of powers.

Section 205: **Joint Powers**

The City shall have the power to contract with any governmental entity, regulated public utility, or other public or private corporation, to perform such services or to acquire, construct, or administer jointly such public works, public utilities, or other facilities, either inside or outside the City limits, as are beneficial to its citizens or the consumers of its utilities.

Section 210: **Administering Oaths; Subpoenas**

Any Council Member, the City Manager, the City Attorney, the City Clerk, or any officer or employee authorized by ordinance, shall have the power to administer oaths and affirmations, and the City Council, either on its own behalf or upon the written request of any City board, commission or committee authorized by ordinance, shall have the power to issue subpoenas, to compel by subpoena the production of books, papers, and documents, and to take and hear testimony or to order the giving of such testimony concerning any matter or thing pending before the Council or such board or commission.

Section 215: **General Laws and Procedures**

The City shall have the power to exercise any and all rights, powers and privileges previously or in the future established, granted or prescribed by the general laws of the state or by other lawful authority and shall have the power to act pursuant to procedure established by any law of the state unless a different procedure is required by this Charter or by ordinance.

Article 3: Officers and Employees

Section 300: Officers and Employees

The officers of the City of Burbank shall be those provided for in this Charter. The Council may provide for such additional boards, commissions, committees, officers, and employees as may be deemed necessary and prescribe their respective powers and duties. The members of the Council shall be elected from the City at large and shall hold office for four (4) years or until their successors are elected and qualified. All other officers, assistants, deputies, clerks, and employees shall be appointed as provided in this Charter, or as the Council may provide by ordinance in case no provision for their appointment is made. They shall hold their respective offices or positions at the pleasure of the appointing power, except as otherwise provided in this Charter. Where the power to appoint is vested in the Council, a three-fifths (3/5) vote of the Council Members shall be required to effect an appointment or removal.

Section 305: The City Council

The legislative body of the City shall consist of five (5) persons elected at large which body shall be known as the Council. The members of the Council shall be elected by the qualified voters of the City in the manner and for the term provided in this Charter. Members of the Council shall receive such compensation as may be prescribed by ordinance but not to exceed the amount which Council Members of general law cities of similar population would receive under State law, nor shall any Council Member be eligible to hold any other office or employment of the City except as may otherwise be provided in this Charter. In the event of resignation such member shall not be entitled to vote on the selection of their successor. Members of the Council shall not hold any other elective public office to which compensation is attached, and the acceptance of any such office or employment shall be deemed a resignation as Council Member.

Section 310: Mayor

The Mayor shall be the executive head of the City. In case of riot, insurrection or extraordinary emergency the Mayor, unless delegated to the City Manager by ordinance, shall assume general control of the City government and all of its branches and be responsible for the suppression of disorders and the restoration of normal conditions. In the name and on behalf of the City the Mayor shall sign all contracts, deeds, bonds and other legal instruments in which the City is a party and countersign all warrants; provided, however, that the Council may by ordinance or resolution authorize any other person to sign the same. The Mayor shall represent the City at all ceremonial functions of a social or patriotic character when it is desirable or appropriate to have the City officially represented. The Mayor shall not receive any compensation for services rendered except that received as a Council Member.

Section 315: City Manager

(A) There shall be a City Manager appointed by the Council who shall be the administrative head of the City government. The City Manager shall be chosen by the Council solely on the basis of the appointee's executive and administrative qualifications with special reference to actual experience in, or knowledge of, accepted practice in respect to the duties of the office.

(B) The City Manager shall be responsible to the Council for the proper administration of all affairs of the City, and to that end, subject to the civil service provisions of this Charter and all applicable laws and regulations, the City Manager shall have power and shall be required to:

    (1) Devote full time to the interests of the City.

(2) Attend all meetings of the council unless excused by the Council or the Mayor, but shall not have a vote.

(3) Appoint and, remove all officers and employees of the City except elected officers and other officers appointed by the Council, and except the employees of such elected officers and other officers appointed by the Council, provided that the City Manager may authorize the head of a department or office to appoint and remove subordinates in such department or office.

(4) Prepare the budget annually and submit it to the Council and be responsible for its administration after adoption by the Council.

(5) Prepare and submit to the Council as of the end of the fiscal year a complete report on the finances and administrative activities of the City for the preceding year.

(6) Keep the Council advised of the financial conditions and future needs of the City and make such recommendations as may seem to be desirable for the consideration and action of the Council.

(7) Perform such other duties as may be prescribed by this Charter or required by the Council, consistent with this Charter.

(8) Be responsible that all ordinances and laws are enforced. It shall be the responsibility and duty of each Department Manager in the City to inform and advise the City Manager of any information indicating lack of law enforcement in the City.

(C) In case of the absence of the City Manager from the City, or of any temporary disability to act as such, the Assistant City Manager or such other person designated by the City Manager shall possess the powers and discharge the duties of the City Manager during such absence or disability. If there is no Assistant City Manager, or no person designated by the City Manager to act in his or her absence or disability, the Council shall appoint a City Manager pro tem, who shall possess the powers and discharge the duties of the City Manager during such absence or disability.

(D) The members of the Council shall not, nor shall any of them, either directly or indirectly, exact from any candidate for the position of City Manager any promise or assurance, or in any way intimate or suggest to such candidate, that such candidate shall, if appointed as City Manager, appoint or employ, or that it is in any way expected the candidate will appoint or employ, any person who has been or may be discussed, mentioned, referred to, approved, or in any way suggested by any member of the Council or other person, as being fit or qualified to have or hold any position in, or do any work for, the City. Nor shall the members or any member of the Council, either directly or indirectly, by suggestion or otherwise, coerce or bring any pressure to bear upon the City Manager, either to appoint any particular person or persons or class of persons to any position that is or may be vacant, or to give employment of any kind to any such persons, or to discharge any person holding any position or doing any work under the City Manager; or to make any purchase of supplies from any particular person, firm or corporation.

The prohibition contained in this Charter shall not be construed to mean that any member of the Council, or other person, shall be prohibited from informing the City Manager as to any fact known to such person which might assist the City Manager in appointing or employing competent, fit, and proper persons, or discharging any incompetent or unfit person previously appointed or employed, or to prohibit the giving of any information which might be of benefit to the City Manager in making an advantageous purchase of materials and supplies.

Section 320:   City Attorney

(A) There shall be a City Attorney appointed by the Council who shall devote full time to the duties of this office and shall not engage in the private practice of law. The City Attorney shall be an attorney-at-law, admitted to the bar of the Supreme Court of this State, and one who has been in actual practice in the State for at least five (5) years directly prior to appointment. The City Attorney shall be the legal adviser of the Council and all other City officials and shall attend all Council meetings unless excused by the Council or the Mayor. The City Attorney shall draft or review all ordinances, contracts, or other legal documents, or proceedings required by the Council or other officials, except as may be otherwise provided, and shall perform such other legal services from time to time as the Council may require.

(B) The Council shall have the power to direct and control the prosecution and defense of all suits and proceedings to which the City is a party, or in which it is interested, and upon the recommendation of the City Attorney, may employ special counsel to assist the City Attorney therein and which the City Attorney shall direct and oversee, and shall provide for the compensation and pay of such counsel.

(C) The City Attorney shall appoint and remove all officers and employees of the City employed in the City Attorney's office subject, when applicable, to the Civil Service system established for the City, and shall do so in keeping with the budget and personnel policies of the City.

**Section 325:		City Clerk**

There shall be a City Clerk elected every four (4) years at the Primary or General Municipal Election who shall be Clerk of the Council.

It shall be a duty of the City Clerk to attend all sessions of the Council and keep a full and correct record of the proceedings thereof. The proceedings of the Council shall be kept in a book marked "Minutes of the Council." The City Clerk shall keep a book marked "Ordinances" in which the City Clerk shall place copies of all City ordinances, certifying that each such copy is a full and correct copy of the original ordinance, and stating that the same has been published as required by law. Said record copy so certified, shall be prima facie evidence of the contents of the ordinance, and of its passage and publication and shall be admissible as such evidence in any court or proceeding. Such record shall not be filed but shall be returned to the custody of the City Clerk. The City Clerk shall also keep a book marked "Resolutions," into which the City Clerk shall place copies of all resolutions passed by the Council. Both the books containing ordinances and resolutions shall be adequately and comprehensively indexed.

The City Clerk shall be the keeper of the corporate seal of the City, and shall affix the same to instruments or writings requiring authentication. The City Clerk shall safely keep all records, documents, ordinances, resolutions, books, and such other papers and matters as may be regularly delivered into the City Clerk's custody or required by law or ordinance to be filed with the City Clerk.

Section 330: **City Treasurer**

There shall be a City Treasurer elected every four (4) years at the Primary or General Municipal election. It shall be the duty of the City Treasurer to receive and safely keep all monies and securities belonging to the City and coming into the City Treasurer's hands, and pay out the same only on warrants signed by the proper officers and not otherwise. The City Treasurer shall hold office for four (4) years and until a successor is elected and qualified.

Section 332: **City Tax Collector**

There shall be a Tax Collector of which office the City Treasurer shall be ex-officio incumbent, unless the Council by ordinance, should provide for the collection of taxes and licenses by some other person or political subdivision of the State of California. The Tax Collector shall perform such duties as may be prescribed by ordinance.

Section 335: **Chief of Police**

There shall be a Chief of Police appointed by the City Manager. The Chief of Police shall be the head of the Police Department of the City, and shall have all the powers that now or in the future may be conferred upon sheriffs and other peace officers by the laws of the state so far as they pertain to the City. It shall be the duty of the Chief of Police to preserve the public peace, to enforce the law and to suppress riots and disturbances. All orders of the Chief of Police shall be promptly executed by the police officers, or members of volunteer law enforcement organizations of the City, and every citizen shall lend aid when requested by the Chief of Police for the arrest of offenders, the maintenance of public order or the protection of life and property.

The Chief of Police shall execute and return all process issued by legal authority. The Chief of Police shall have the duty and the authority to arrest persons violating any laws of the nation, state, county or City. The Chief of Police shall have such other powers and duties pertaining to this office as may be prescribed by the Council or rules of the Police Department.

Section 340:   Fire Chief

There shall be a Fire Chief appointed by the City Manager. The Fire Chief shall be head of the Fire Department of the City, and shall have charge and supervision over all matters relating to the prevention and extinguishment of fires, and of all measures necessary to guard and protect all persons and property impaired thereby. During the time of a fire the Fire Chief shall always have supreme authority over the territory involved in and around such fire, and all persons in the immediate vicinity of the fire during such time, including police officers, shall be subject to the Fire Chief's orders.

Section 370:   Official Bonds

The Council shall, by ordinance, determine which officers and employees shall be subject to group or individual bonds to insure faithful performance of their official and ex-officio duties, shall fix the amount of such bonds and provide for the payment of premiums by the City.

Section 375:   Oath of Office

Every officer shall take the constitutional oath or affirmation of office and sign such oath or affirmation before entering upon the performance of any official duties.

Section 380: Additional Duties of Officers

Besides the duties specified in this Charter, all officers and boards shall perform such other appropriate duties as may be prescribed by ordinance or the general laws.

Section 385: Compensation

The Council, except as otherwise provided in this Charter, shall fix the compensation of all officers appointed by the Council.

The City Manager shall fix the compensation of all deputies, assistants and employees of all officers appointed by or under the authority of the City Manager subject to the approval of the Council.

The City Attorney and elected officials shall fix the compensation of all deputies, assistants and employees of the City employed in their offices subject to the budget and the personnel policies of the City, and subject to the approval of the Council.

Section 390: Employees' Retirement System

(A) The "Public Employees' Retirement Law" (hereafter in this section, "Retirement Law") as now existing or as in the future may be amended, is hereby adopted for the City of Burbank.

(B) All necessary authority and power is hereby vested in the City, its Council and its officers, agents and employees to do and perform any act, or exercise any authority granted, permitted, or required under the provisions of the Retirement Law, to enable the City to become and remain a contracting City participating in the Public Employees' Retirement System.

(C) The contract entered into shall provide for the participation of all full time employees (except temporary and/or seasonal employees) of the City working under the personnel system and of all full time elective and appointive officers of the City, and the contract shall give full credit for prior services rendered by the employees and full time elective and appointive officers to the City of Burbank prior to the effective date of the contract and shall provide compulsory retirement as provided in the Retirement Law.

(D) The Council may terminate any contract entered into with the Board of Administration of the Public Employees' Retirement System only under authority granted by an ordinance adopted by a majority vote of the electors of the City of Burbank.

Section 395: **Civil Service System**

The Council shall provide for the establishment of a Civil Service System in the City of Burbank based on merit and suitability.

Article 4: Meetings of the Council

Section 400: Meetings, Regular and Special

The Council shall meet at 10:00 a.m. on the first day of May following their election or if such day be a Saturday, Sunday or holiday, then upon the next regular working day. The new members shall then be inducted into office, whereupon the Council, as thus newly constituted, shall choose one of their member to serve as Mayor. The Mayor shall have the same voting power as any other member of the Council. The Council shall also choose one of their member to serve as Vice Mayor, who shall act as Mayor pro tempore in case of the absence, sickness or other disability of the Mayor. The officials so chosen shall hold their respective offices subject to the pleasure of the Council. The regular meetings of the Council shall be held at least twice per month and such further regular meetings shall be held as determined by ordinance. The time for holding all regular meetings of the Council shall be provided for by ordinance or resolution, but any regular meeting may be adjourned to a time certain, which adjourned meeting shall be a regular meeting for all purposes.

Special meetings may be called as provided by the laws of the State of California.

Except as otherwise provided by State law, all meetings of the Council shall be open to the public and held in the City Hall or such other place as may be prescribed by ordinance or resolution, unless the Council is compelled to meet elsewhere by reason of fire, flood, earthquake, other emergency, or the temporary unavailability of the regular meeting place. The Council shall adopt rules for conducting its proceedings.

Section 405:   Public Participation

During any meeting of the Council, all persons are encouraged to address the Council on any item that is within the subject matter jurisdiction of the City Council or as otherwise required by state law. The Council shall provide for a reasonable period of comment consistent with the completion of the public's business, and may punish any member or other person for disorderly behavior at any meeting.

Section 410:   Quorum

A majority of the Council Members shall constitute a quorum for the transaction of any business, but a lesser number may adjourn from time to time and compel the attendance of absent members in such manner and under such penalties as may be prescribed by ordinance.

Article 5: Council Actions and Enactments

Section 500: Ordinances, Resolutions or Motions

The Council may take official action only by the passage or adoption of ordinances, resolutions or motions, as may be prescribed by the Constitution or Laws of the State of California, and the provisions of this Charter; provided that any action of the Council fixing or prescribing a fine, punishment or penalty, or granting any franchise, shall be taken by ordinance. In the absence of any express provision to the contrary in the California Constitution, Laws or Charter, the Council may choose any of the above three methods of taking such action. All proposed ordinances introduced in the Council shall be in printed form. The enacting clause of all ordinances passed by the Council shall read as follows:

"The Council of the City of Burbank does ordain as follows:"

The affirmative vote of not less than three (3) members of the Council shall be necessary to adopt any ordinances, resolutions or approve or reject claims against the City, which vote shall be taken by ayes and noes and entered upon the minutes of the Council.

Except as provided in this Charter no ordinance shall be passed by the Council on the day of its introduction, nor within five (5) days thereafter. Every ordinance shall be read in full only when requested by a majority of the Council. A proposed ordinance may be amended or modified between the time of its introduction and the time of its final passage, providing its general scope and original purpose are retained. All ordinances shall be signed by the Mayor and attested by the City Clerk, and the City Attorney's synopsis of such ordinances shall be published at least once in a newspaper of general circulation within fourteen (14) days of adoption, and shall become effective at 12:01 a.m. on the 31st day from and after the date of the adoption, and in computing such time the day of adoption shall be excluded; provided, however, that an ordinance calling or otherwise relating to an election, or ordinances otherwise specially required by the laws of the State, or ordinances declared by the Council to be necessary as an emergency measure for preserving the public peace, health, safety or welfare or as mandated by a state or federal law, regulation, or permit condition, and containing the reasons for its urgency and passed by not less than four (4) members of the Council, or ordinances relating to bond issues, may be introduced and passed at one and the same meeting, and shall become effective immediately, if the Council shall in such ordinance so provide and shall be published in a newspaper of general circulation within fourteen (14) days following adoption. However, no measure creating or abolishing any office or changing the salaries, terms or duties of any office or creating any franchise or special privilege or creating any vested right or interest shall be construed to be an emergency or urgency measure.

Section 505:   Adoption of Codes by Reference

The duly adopted and effective ordinances of the City, when compiled, arranged and codified or re-codified, may be adopted by reference by passage of an ordinance for such purpose. Detailed regulations not embodied in any ordinance, such as fire, building, plumbing, electrical, and heating and cooling codes, as well as codes on other subjects, may be enacted in the same manner. Amendments to such codes shall be adopted by the same procedures as amendments to ordinances generally. Copies of all codes adopted by reference, that are not commercially available for sale, shall be made available to the public at a reasonable price.

Article 6: City Departments and Governmental Functions

Section 600: Governmental Functions

In addition to public safety services and water and electric utility services, the City of Burbank, as a well managed and balanced City, shall serve the following functions:

(1) Plan for and initiate sustainable long-range physical, economic, and social development of the City.

(2) Effectively manage and maintain the City's infrastructure, including street, traffic, and transportation systems; sanitary and refuse systems; and public facilities.

(3) Ensure open access to and availability of information and knowledge.

(4) Provide high quality recreation facilities, programs, and activities designed to meet the human service, recreational, social, cultural, and educational needs of the City's constituents.

(5) Provide high quality administrative support services designed to help the City meet its constituents' needs in an effective and efficient manner, including human resources, information management, budgeting, accounting, and other operations.

(6) Such other functions as determined by the Council which are not prohibited by the California Constitution or this Charter.

Section 605: Department Structure

Any department or function provided for in this Charter or by ordinance, may be subsequently combined with other divisions or departments, redivided, or otherwise reorganized at the discretion of the City Manager.

Section 610: **Utility Department**

There shall be a Utility Department to be known as Burbank Water and Power and a General Manager appointed by the City Manager.

The Department shall supervise the construction, reconstruction, operation and maintenance of all public utilities now or hereafter owned and operated by the City, including, but not limited to, the generation, purchase, distribution and sale of electric energy, water, gas, and telecommunications services and may, with the approval of the Council, lease or rent any property connected with any of its utilities and fix the rental charges thereof.

All funds received by the City related to the Department shall be deposited in the City Treasury to the credit of the Department. An amount not to exceed two percent (2%) of the Department's gross sales of electricity (exclusive of wholesale sales of electricity to other public or privately owned utilities) shall, in the Council's discretion, be deposited or transferred to the City's General fund, or pay bills incurred by the City for lighting its public streets, and an amount not to exceed five percent (5%) of the Department's gross sales of water and electricity, in lieu of taxes (exclusive of wholesale sales to other public or privately owned utilities) shall be deposited or transferred to the City's General Fund at the discretion of the Council.

Funds not immediately needed by the Department may be temporarily loaned to other departments of the City pending collection of tax receipts or other funds owing to such other department.

Article 7: Boards, Commissions and Committees

Section 700: Boards, Commissions and Committees

The Council may from time to time establish boards, commissions and committees, both ad hoc and standing, to advise the City and the Council on matters of public concern. In addition to any other boards, commissions and committees, there shall be the Planning Board, the Parks, Recreation and Community Services Board, the Civil Service Board, the Burbank Water and Power Board, and the Library Board, the size, membership and duties of each to be determined by the Council.

Section 705: Police Commission

(A) There shall be a Police Commission, the size and membership of which are to be determined by the Council.

(B) The Police Commission shall have the following powers and duties:

> **(1)** To initiate studies and surveys in the general field of police science and law enforcement and report its findings and recommendations to the Council;
>
> **(2)** To conduct hearings, investigations, or both, at the request of the Council for the purpose of ascertaining whether additional legislation is needed for the health, safety, peace and welfare of the inhabitants of the City and to make findings and recommendations to the Council;
>
> **(3)** To act in an advisory capacity to the Council on policy matters pertaining to the Police Department of the City;

(4) To receive complaints, except those relating to traffic engineering, pertaining to the Police Department and law enforcement in general;

(5) To examine books, papers, records and accounts in the Police Department, other than confidential matters under investigation.

(C) The Council or the City Manager may assign other powers and duties to the Commission as they shall deem appropriate.

Article 8:   Elections

Section 800:   Elections

Municipal elections held in the City of Burbank shall be classified as of three (3) kinds:

(1)   Primary Nominating Elections

(2)   General Municipal Elections

(3)   Special Elections

Primary Nominating Elections shall be held on the last Tuesday in February in every odd-numbered year, and general municipal elections shall be held on the second Tuesday in April in every odd-numbered year, except that if either of said days is a legal holiday such election shall be held on the following day. The officers elected at a Primary or General Municipal election shall, after they have qualified, enter upon the discharge of the duties of their offices, on the first day of May following their election and shall hold office for the period of four (4) years or until their successors are elected and qualified.

Candidates to be voted for at any General Municipal Election shall be nominated at a Primary Nominating Election. No person shall be eligible to be nominated for an elective office of the City unless such person has resided in the City for at least twenty-nine (29) days prior to filing nomination papers or a declaration of candidacy, and such person is a registered voter of the City at the time of nomination or election to office, whichever is sooner; and no names shall be printed upon the ballot for such general election other than those selected in the manner prescribed in this Charter.

Whenever possible the officers of election who shall be appointed for the Primary Nominating Election shall be the officers of election of such General Municipal Election and such General Municipal Election shall be held at the same places as far as possible, and the polls shall be opened and closed at the same hours, as may be provided for Primary Nominating Elections. In the event that any candidate for nomination to any office for which only one (1) person is to be elected shall receive a majority of the votes cast for all candidates for nomination to such office at such Primary Nominating Election, the candidate so receiving such majority vote shall be deemed to be and declared by the Council to be elected to such office; provided, that in the case of candidates for the offices of Member of the Council and Member of the Board of Education, the candidates which are equal to or less than the number of such offices for which nominations are to be made who receive a majority of the votes of the voters voting for such office shall be deemed to be and declared by the Council to be elected to such office or offices, and their names shall not be printed upon the ballot to be used at the following general election.

Except as provided above, the two (2) candidates receiving the highest number of votes for any given office at the Primary Nominating Election shall be the candidates, and the only candidates, for such office whose names shall be printed upon the ballots to be used at the General Municipal Election; provided, that where more than one (1) office of the same kind is to be filled, the candidates for such offices, equaling in number twice the number of such offices, who receive the highest number of votes at the Primary Nominating Election, shall be the candidates, and the only candidates, for such offices whose names shall be printed upon the ballot to be used at such general election.

Whenever it shall appear upon the canvass of the returns of either a primary or general election that two (2) or more persons have received an equal number of votes as candidates for any office at such election, so that the result of such election does not determine which of such persons has been nominated for or elected to such office, the City Clerk shall notify in writing all such persons so receiving such equal vote to appear before the Council at the time specified in the notice. Such persons shall appear before the Council at such time and place and then and there, in open session, draw lots, in such manner as the Council shall prescribe, to determine which of such persons shall be nominated for or elected to such office. If any such persons shall not so appear, the City Clerk shall act for such person or persons in such drawing of lots.

All municipal elections shall, except as in this Charter otherwise provided, be conducted and held in substantial accordance with the provisions of the laws of the state for holding of municipal elections except as otherwise provided by the City Election Code. No amendments to the City Elections Code shall be effective during the six (6) months immediately preceding any General Municipal Election in the City of Burbank, nor during the period between the ordering and the holding of a special election.

The Council shall have power to submit to the voters of the City at any election any proposition or question or ordinance required or authorized to be so submitted by the Constitution of the State of California, the law, this Charter, or by ordinance; provided, that in case such proposition or question is required by the Constitution, law, Charter, or ordinance to be submitted at a special or other particular kind of election, it shall be so submitted, and not otherwise.

Except as otherwise provided in this Charter, every special election shall be ordered, held and conducted (except as to the date of such election) and the result made known and declared in the same manner as provided in this Charter for other elections. The Council may consolidate special elections with each other or with any municipal, county or state election. When any elections shall have been consolidated as provided in this Charter, they shall be held, conducted, the returns canvassed and the result declared in all particulars the same as one election. Provided, that when any municipal election is consolidated with any state or county election, the ballots used may be the ballots used at such state or county election, or may be separate ballots, or the voting may be in such manner as may be authorized by law, and the appropriate officials of the County of Los Angeles shall canvass the returns and shall certify the result of such canvass of all municipal questions submitted at such election, to the Council, who shall thereupon declare the result, and any act in relation to the conduct of such election, required by this Charter to be performed by any officer or employee of the City, shall be performed by the proper officer or employee of the County.

The Council shall, by ordinance, order the holding of all elections. Every such ordinance shall specify the object and time of holding any such election. Such ordinance shall also direct the City Clerk to publish, not later than twenty (20) days prior to an election, a list of election precincts, polling places, and election officers for each precinct. The ordinance shall also set forth the places of posting by the City Clerk of three (3) copies of such list of election precincts, polling places and election officers in three public places in the City, and such lists shall so remain until the day after such election. When two (2) or more municipal elections are consolidated by the Council, it shall not be necessary to set forth the precincts, polling places and election officers in more than one (1) list. If a municipal election is consolidated with a State or County election, it shall not be necessary to set forth the precincts, polling places, or election officers, but reference shall be made to the notice, resolution, or ordinance of the Board of Supervisors of Los Angeles County calling such election and fixing precincts, polling places and election officers. All ordinances ordering the holding or consolidation of elections shall be published once in a newspaper of general circulation at least five (5) days prior to the date of such election.

The Council may conduct any City election by all mail ballot in accordance with provisions adopted by ordinance. In such elections any inconsistent provisions of this Charter shall not be applicable.

Section 805: **Canvass of Returns**

The City Clerk shall begin canvassing the returns at eight o'clock, A.M. on the second working day after all of the returns from any municipal election have been received in the City Clerk's office. Such canvass shall be publicly conducted and continued until completed.

Whenever requested by the City Clerk, the Council shall authorize the temporary employment of such persons in addition to the persons regularly employed in the City Clerk's office, as may be necessary to assist the City Clerk in the performance of any duty imposed by the Charter or by the Council in connection with the conduct of any election.

The City Clerk shall post the results of such election in three (3) public places within the City. Within five (5) days after such posting, any registered voter of the City may file a verified written protest with the City Clerk contesting the count of the ballots. The protest shall set forth specifically the following:

(1) The elector's name and address.

(2) The name of the person whose right to be nominated or elected for an office, stating the office, is being contested; or the proposition being contested.

(3) The number of the precinct or precincts in which it is contested errors in the counting of ballots would, if corrected, give a different result.

(4) A statement of particulars as to the errors claimed to have been made in the original count.

(5) A demand for a recount of the ballots cast at such election in the specified precinct or precincts.

(6) A deposit in an amount estimated by the City Clerk to cover the cost of the recount.

The City Clerk shall present the result of the canvass of the returns of the election, together with any and all protests, to the Council at its next regular meeting after the expiration of the time for filing such protests. Unless a protest has been filed, the Council shall accept the canvass of returns by the City Clerk as correct and shall publicly declare the result. When any such protest has been filed, the Council shall fix a time for such recount, not more than seven (7) days following the Council meeting, for the City Clerk to conduct a recount of the ballots in the specified precinct or precincts only and as to the specified office or proposition. Upon the completion of such recount the Council shall publicly declare the result. The action of the Council shall be final.

The Council shall be the judge of the qualifications of all the elective officers of the City.

Section 810: **Qualification for Elective Office**

No person may assume or hold an elective office of the City unless he or she is a registered voter of the City.

Section 815: **Initiative, Referendum and Recall**

The provisions of the Elections Code of the State of California governing the exercise of the powers of initiative and referendum in cities and governing the exercise of the power of recall of municipal officers shall apply to the exercise of those powers in the City insofar as such provisions may be applicable and except as otherwise provided in this Charter, or as otherwise provided by the Council by ordinance.

Article 9: Vacancies

Section 900:   Vacancies

(A)   A vacancy in the office of Council Member from whatever cause shall be filled by appointment by the Council, such appointee to hold office until the next regularly scheduled municipal election; provided that if the Council fails to agree or for any other reason does not fill such vacancy within thirty (30) days after the same occurs, then such vacancy shall be filled by the Mayor. Should a vacancy occur after the opening of the filing period for election to the office of Council Member, or within thirty (30) days before the beginning of such filing period, then the appointee shall hold office until the regularly scheduled election next following the one for which the filing period is called. Should the appointment be for an unexpired term which has two or more years remaining when the next regularly scheduled election occurs, then the candidate elected who receives the lesser number of votes, shall be deemed elected to the remaining term for which the appointment was made.

(B)   If the seats of a majority of the Council shall become vacant, then the City Clerk shall call a special election at once to fill the vacancies for the unexpired terms and the same shall be conducted substantially in the manner provided for General Municipal Elections, and the candidates receiving the greatest number of votes, equal to the number of vacancies, shall be deemed elected.

(C)   A vacancy on the Council shall occur if any member of the Council shall fail to attend any regular meeting of the Council for sixty (60) consecutive days without the permission of the Council, or shall fail to qualify, or shall move their place of residence outside the City, or shall cease to be an elector of the City, or shall resign, or be convicted of a felony, or be adjudged mentally incompetent.

Article 10: Finances and Budget

Section 1000: Fiscal Year

The fiscal year of the City shall commence on the first day of July of each year, or at such other time as may be fixed by ordinance.

Section 1005: Budget

On or before the first day of June the City Manager shall prepare, or have prepared, a proposed budget and submit it to the City Council with appropriate recommendations. The budget shall include estimates of the sources and uses of available funds for the following fiscal year. These estimates shall be compiled from detailed information obtained from the various departments. Terminology and classifications used shall be uniform in accordance with generally accepted accounting practices. The budget shall include:

(1) An itemization of all anticipated revenues of the City.

(2) A statement of the proposed use of funds for the following fiscal year.

(3) Comparisons of current and prior year sources and uses of the funds.

(4) The total amount of City debt outstanding.

(5) A statement of the amounts which should be appropriated to pay all principal and interest payments on debts of the City and all its related entities.

(6) An item to be known as "unappropriated balance" which sum shall be available for appropriation later in the fiscal year to meet contingencies which might arise.

(7) A capital budget of proposed activities, developments, and improvements listed by category and specifying the anticipated sources of funding.

(8) Such other information as may be required by the Council or which the City Manager may deem advisable to submit. Sufficient copies of the proposed budget shall be prepared and printed that there be one (1) copy furnished each member of the Council and the City Clerk shall have sufficient copies for the inspection of the public. The Council may also provide for the printing and issuing of the adopted budget.

The Council shall have the power to revise, correct, or modify the proposed budget in any particular.

After considering the proposed budget, the Council shall fix a time for holding a public hearing upon the proposed budget and shall publish notice of the time fixed for the hearing one (1) time in a newspaper of general circulation at least ten (10) days before the time of the hearing. After the hearing, the Council may further modify or correct the proposed budget, and shall by resolution, adopted by a majority of the members of the Council adopt the budget, and authorize the tax levy required to provide funding for those uses identified for the fiscal year less the amounts to be raised by bond issues and revenues collected or transferred from other sources.

At any meeting after the adoption of the budget, the Council, by majority vote, may amend or supplement the budget so as to authorize the transfer of unused balances appropriated for one purpose to another, or to appropriate available revenue not included in the annual budget at its passage.

Section 1010: **Municipal Bonded Indebtedness**

The incurring of any general obligation bonded indebtedness of the City shall require the votes of two thirds (2/3) of the voters voting at a special election to be held for that purpose; provided, however, that when two (2) or more propositions for incurring any bonded indebtedness are submitted at the same election the votes cast for and against each proposition shall be counted separately and when two thirds (2/3) of the voters voting on any one of such propositions vote in favor thereof such proposition shall be deemed adopted. Such special election may be consolidated with any municipal, county, state or other election.

Before or at the time of incurring such bonded indebtedness, provision shall be made as required by the Constitution of the State of California for the collection of an annual tax sufficient to pay the interest on such bonded indebtedness as it falls due and also to constitute a sinking fund for the payment of the principal on or before maturity. The Council may at any time use, for the payment of principal or interest of such bonds, revenues derived from sales or use taxes or any other revenues or income of the City not allocated to, set aside for, or required to be used for a special purpose or constituting a special or trust fund.

The provisions of this section shall not apply to revenue bonds issued pursuant to the provisions of the laws of the State of California or procedural ordinance of the City and payable solely from the revenues of a revenue producing system or facility of the City, and nothing in this section or elsewhere in this Charter shall authorize the use of any revenues of any revenue producing system or facility of the City in any manner or for any purpose contrary to a covenant or agreement contained in any ordinance, resolution or other proceeding (whether taken or adopted before or subsequent to the adoption of this section) authorizing the issuance of revenue bonds payable from the revenues of such revenue producing system or facility.

Section 1015: Deposits With Treasurer

All moneys collected for the City by an officer or department thereof shall be paid into the treasury daily at the direction of the City Treasurer.

Section 1020: Payment of City Funds

Despite any other provisions of this Charter, demands against the City shall be presented, numbered and allowed or disallowed and warrants shall be numbered, dated, issued and signed as prescribed by ordinance. No demand shall be allowed, approved, audited or paid unless it shall specify each item of the claim and the date submitted.

Section 1025: Surplus Bond Money

All moneys derived from the sale of bonds, including premiums and accrued interest, shall be applied only to the purposes for which the bonds were voted. After such purposes have been fully completed and paid for, any remaining surplus shall be transferred to the bond interest and redemption fund.

Section 1030: Uniform Accounts and Reports

The City shall use a uniform chart of accounts, which shall be observed by all officers and departments of the City which receive or disburse City moneys.

Section 1035: Independent Auditor

The Council shall employ an independent certified public accounting firm to annually provide a full scope audit of the books and records of all funds and entities of the City of Burbank, and present its report to the City.

Section 1040: **Financial Reports**

Annual audited financial reports shall be submitted to the Council by the City Manager in such form as may be approved by the Council, and monthly financial reports shall be maintained by and available for public inspection in the Financial Services Department.

Section 1045: **Approving Illegal Claims**

Every officer who shall willfully and knowingly approve, allow or pay any demand on the treasury not authorized by law, shall be liable to the City individually and on such officer's official bond for the amount of the demand so approved, allowed or paid, and shall forfeit such office and be forever disbarred and disqualified from holding any position in the service of the City.

Article 11: Board of Education

Section 1100: **Board of Education**

(A) The control of the public schools of the City of Burbank, including the whole of the Burbank Unified School District, shall be vested in a Board of Education, which shall consist of five (5) members elected at large.

(B) The members of the Board of Education shall be elected in the manner provided by this Charter and shall serve for a term of four (4) years.

(C) The powers and duties of the Board of Education shall be such as are prescribed by the Constitution and laws of the State of California, and shall include the power to submit to the voters at any election any proposition or question required or authorized to be so submitted by the Constitution of the State of California, the law, or by this Charter; provided, that in case such proposition or question is required by the Constitution, law, or Charter, to be submitted at a special or other particular kind of election, it shall be so submitted, and not otherwise.

Article 12: Purchasing, Contracts, Franchises, Improvements and Property

Section 1200: Public Improvements and Street Work

All public improvements, including the improving, widening, opening, extending, and closing of streets, lanes, or alleys, may be done and made in pursuance of the general laws of the state or procedure ordinances adopted by the Council or the voters, and the whole or any portion of the cost of such improvements paid out of the City treasury or assessed on the property fronting on the improvement, or the district or lands benefited.

Section 1205: Contract Work and Purchases

(A) Contract Work

Every contract involving an expenditure of City moneys over an amount set by Ordinance for public works construction shall be let to the lowest responsible bidder after notice by publication in a newspaper of general circulation by two (2) insertions, the first of which shall be at least ten (10) days before the time for opening bids. In the case of an emergency, as established by Ordinance, such contracts may be awarded without advertising for bids and without Council approval. The Council shall have the right to waive any informality or minor irregularity in a bid. The City Manager may reject any and all bids presented and, in his or her discretion, may re-advertise for bids, or recommend to the Council to dispense with competitive bidding. If the Council determines to dispense with competitive bidding, it shall do so by resolution, finding that it is in the best interests of the City.

(B) Purchases of Supplies, Materials, Equipment and Services Generally

Before making any purchase of, or contract for, supplies, materials, equipment or services (other than professional or contractual services which are, in their nature, unique and not subject to competitive bidding), the City Manager or a designated representative shall provide for competitive bidding under such definitions, conditions, terms, rules and regulations and with such exceptions as the Council shall prescribe by ordinance.

Section 1210: Illegal and Void Contracts

No officer or employee of the City shall have an interest in any contract or be the purchaser at any sale or the vendor at any purchase to which the City is a party, except to the extent permitted by state law as now or hereafter provided.
No officer or employee of the City shall aid or assist a bidder in securing a contract to furnish labor, material or supplies at a higher price or rate than that proposed by any other bidder, or favor one bidder over another, giving or withholding information or willfully mislead any bidder in regard to the character of the materials or supplies called for, or knowingly accept materials or supplies of a quality inferior to that called for by the contract, or knowingly certify to a greater amount of labor performed than has actually been performed, or to the receipt of a greater amount of material or supplies than has actually been received. If at any time it shall be found that the person, firm or corporation to whom a contract has been awarded has, in presenting any bid or bids, colluded with any other party or parties, then the contract so awarded shall, if the City so elect, be null and void and the contractor and its bondsmen shall be liable to the City for all loss or damage which the City may suffer due to such violation. In that event the Council may advertise again for bids for the work or supplies.

Any officer or employee violating any of the provisions of this section shall be guilty of a misdemeanor and shall be immediately expelled from office or employment by the officer or board responsible for employment, and the contract or transaction may be voided at the option of the Council.

Section 1215: **Franchises**

Every franchise or privilege to construct, maintain, or operate any railroad, or other means of transportation in or over any street or highway, or to lay pipes or conduits, or erect poles or wires or other structures in or across any street or highway for the transmission of gas, electricity, or other commodity, or for the use of public property or places now or hereafter belonging to the City, shall be granted under and in pursuance of the provisions of this Charter, any applicable City ordinances, resolutions or policies and the general laws of the state relating to the granting of such franchises or privileges. The Council may place any condition on such franchise or privilege consistent with the California Constitution, general laws and this Charter.

Section 1220: **Disposition of Real Property**

Any real property owned by the City of Burbank which has been or which may be dedicated to City use, and which is determined by a majority of the Council to be unsuitable or impractical for continued City use, may be sold or leased, either in whole or in part, under such terms and conditions and such procedure as the Council may by ordinance prescribe; and the proceeds of such sale or lease shall be paid into the City Treasury.

Article 13:   Official Records and Official Notices

Section 1300:   Official Records

The right to inspect public records of the City and to obtain copies thereof or information therefrom shall be governed by the laws of the State of California.

All officers and boards shall deliver to their successors all papers, books, documents, records, archives and other properties pertaining to their respective offices or departments, in their possession or under their control.

Section 1305:   Newspaper Advertising

The publication of all ordinances and other legal notices of the City shall be made in a newspaper of general circulation published in the County of Los Angeles which has a substantial distribution to paid subscribers in the City, unless otherwise required by law.

The publication of every ordinance shall be complete if a notice of the ordinance is published which contains the full title, number and date of the ordinance, a brief synopsis of the content of the ordinance and the statement that a copy of the ordinance is on file and available for public inspection in the office of the City Clerk.

Article 14: Amendment

Section 1400: **Charter Amendments**

This Charter may be amended pursuant to the procedure set forth in the Constitution and laws of this state.
Not more than five (5) years following completion of the previous Charter review or the completion of the citizen committee review as provided in this paragraph, whichever is most recent, the Council shall appoint a citizen committee of five (5) members, one (1) appointed by each Council Member, to consider the Charter and advise the Council whether a comprehensive Charter review is necessary. The committee may recommend a full review, a limited, focused review, or no review. Upon such recommendation the Council may appoint a full Charter Review Committee, the number and appointments of which shall be determined by the Council, to determine what, if any, Charter changes should be placed before the voters.

From time to time the Council may also place other proposed Charter changes before the voters.

Article 15: Continuation of Previous Ordinances and Contracts; Constitutionality

Section 1500:   **Continuing Ordinances in Force**

All lawful ordinances, resolutions and regulations in force at the time this Charter shall take effect, and which are consistent with its provisions, are hereby continued in force until they shall have been duly amended, repealed or superseded.

Section 1505:   **Continuing Contracts in Force**

All vested rights of the City shall continue and shall not in any manner be affected by the adoption of this Charter; nor shall any right, liability, pending suit or prosecution, either in behalf of or against the City, be affected by the adoption of this Charter. All contracts entered into by the City prior to the taking effect of this Charter shall continue in full force and effect. All public work begun prior to the taking effect of this Charter shall be continued and completed.

Section 1510:   **Constitutional Clause**

If any section, subsection, sentence, clause or phrase of this Charter is for any reason held to be unconstitutional, such decision shall not affect the validity of the remaining portions of this Charter. The people of the City of Burbank hereby declare that they would have ratified and adopted, and the Legislature hereby declares that it would have approved this Charter and each section, subsection, sentence, clause and phrase of this Charter, irrespective of the fact that any one or more other sections, subsections, sentences, clauses or phrases be declared unconstitutional.

**The Home Rule Charter of
The City of Carlsbad, California**

Table of Contents

Preamble **Page 62**

Article 1: **Municipal Affairs** **Page 63**

Section 100: Powers of City

Section 101: Municipal Affairs; Generally

Section 102: Incorporation and Succession

Article 2: **Form of Government** **Page 65**

Section 200: Form of Government

Article 3: **Local Limits of Growth Control** **Page 66**

Section 300: Local Limits of Growth Control

Article 4: **Revenue, Savings and Generation** **Page 67**

Section 400: Economic and Community Development

Section 401: Public Financing

Section 402: Utility Franchises

Section 403: Enterprises

Section 404: Contracts

Article 5:	**Revenue Retention**	**Page 69**

Section 500: Reductions Prohibited

Section 501: Mandates Limited

Section 502: Retention of Benefits

Article 6:	**General Laws**	**Page 70**

Section 600: General Law Powers

Article 7:	**Interpretation**	**Page 71**

Section 700: Construction and Interpretation

Section 701: Severability

Article 8:	**Amendment**	**Page 72**

Section 800: Amendment to Charter, Revised or Repealed

Preamble

We the people of the City of Carlsbad, declare our intent to maintain in our community the historic principles of self-governance inherent in the doctrine of home-rule. We the people of Carlsbad, are sincerely committed to the belief that local government has the closest affinity to the people governed and firmly convinced that the economic and fiscal independence of our local government will better serve and promote the health, safety and welfare of all the citizens of Carlsbad. Based on these principles, we do hereby exercise the express right granted by the Constitution of the State of California and do ordain and establish this Charter for the City of Carlsbad.

Article 1: Municipal Affairs

Section 100: **Powers of City**

The City shall have full power and authority to adopt, make, exercise and enforce all legislation, laws and regulations with respect to municipal affairs, subject only to the limitations and restrictions as may be provided in this Charter, in the Constitution of the State of California, and in the laws of the United States.

Section 101: **Municipal Affairs; Generally**

Each of the matters set forth in this Charter are declared to be municipal affairs, consistent with the laws of the State of California. The implementation of each matter uniquely benefits the citizens of the City of Carlsbad and addresses peculiarly local concerns within the City of Carlsbad. The municipal affairs set forth in this Charter are not intended to be an exclusive list of municipal affairs over which the City Council may govern.

Section 102: **Incorporation and Succession**

The City of Carlsbad shall continue to be a municipal corporation known as the City of Carlsbad. The boundaries of the City of Carlsbad shall continue as now established until changed in the manner authorized by law. The City of Carlsbad shall remain vested with and shall continue to own, have, possess, control and enjoy all property rights and rights of action of every nature and description owned, had, possessed, controlled or enjoyed by it at the time this Charter takes affect. The City of Carlsbad shall be subject to all debts, obligations and liabilities of the City of Carlsbad at the time this Charter takes effect. All lawful ordinances, resolutions, rules and regulations, or portions thereof, enforced at the time this Charter takes effect and not in conflict with or inconsistent herewith, are hereby continued in force until the same have been duly repealed, amended, changed or superseded by proper lawful action.

Article 2:   Form of Government

Section 200:   **Form of Government**

The municipal government established by this Charter shall be known as the "Council-Manager" form of government. The City Council shall establish the policy of the City; the City Manager shall carry out that policy.

Article 3: Local Limits of Growth Control

Section 300:   Local Limits of Growth Control

The citizens of Carlsbad recognize and declare that managing and limiting growth and ensuring that necessary public facilities are provided to the citizens of the City of Carlsbad are quintessential elements of local control and therefore are municipal affairs. The adoption of this Charter recognizes and reaffirms the principles of the growth management program established by the citizens as Proposition E in 1986 and affirms the principle that this program, that implements a municipal affair shall be superior to and take precedence over any conflicting general laws of the State of California. The intent of this Charter is to allow the City Council and the voters to exercise the maximum degree of control over land use matters within the City of Carlsbad.

Article 4: Revenue, Savings and Generation

Section 400: Economic and Community Development

Subject to the expenditure limitation established by the citizens of Carlsbad Proposition H in 1982, the City shall have the power to utilize revenues from the general fund to encourage, support and promote economic and community development in the City.

Section 401: Public Financing

The City Council shall have the power to establish standards, procedures, rules and regulations relating to financing of public improvements and services.

Section 402: Utility Franchises

The City Council shall have the power to provide for the acquisition, development or operation by the City of any public utility and/or to grant any franchise, license or permit to any public utility which proposes to use or is using City streets, highways or other rights-of-way.

Section 403: Enterprises

The City shall have the power to engage in any enterprise determined necessary to produce revenues for the general fund or any other fund established by the City Council that promotes a public purpose.

Section 404: **Contracts**

The City Council shall have the power to establish standards, procedures, rules or regulations relating to all aspects of the award and performance of contracts, including contracts for the construction of public improvements, including, but not limited to, compensation paid for performance of such work.

Article 5: Revenue Retention

Section 500: Reductions Prohibited

All revenues due to, and raised by the City, shall remain within the City of Carlsbad for appropriation solely by the City Council. No such revenue shall be subject to subtraction, retention, attachment, withdrawal or any other form of involuntary reduction by any other level of government.

Section 501: Mandates Limited

No person, whether elected or appointed, acting on behalf of the City, shall be required to implement or give effect to, any function which is mandated by any other level of government, unless and until funds sufficient for the performance of such function are provided by such other level of government.

Section 502: Retention of Benefits

Safety employees hired on or after October 4, 2010 and miscellaneous employees hired after November 27, 2011 (the effective date of the ordinances amending the City's contracts with CalPERS to create a second tier of retirement benefits for safety and miscellaneous employees) shall not have their retirement benefit formulas (commonly known as the 2% at 50 years of age or 2% at 60 year of age formulas respectively) increased without an amendment to this section. The City Council may reduce this formula as provided in state law without an amendment to this section.

Article 6: General Laws

Section 600: General Law Powers

In addition to the power and authority granted by the terms of this Charter and the Constitution of the State of California, the City shall have the power and authority to adopt, make, exercise and enforce all legislation, laws, and regulations and to take all actions and to exercise any and all rights, powers and privileges heretofore or hereafter established, granted or prescribed by any law of the State of California or by any other lawful authority. In the event of any conflict between the provisions of this Charter and the provisions of the general laws of the State of California, the provisions of this Charter shall control.

Article 7: Interpretation

Section 700: **Construction and Interpretation**

The language contained in this Charter is intended to be permissive rather than exclusive or limiting and shall be liberally and broadly construed in favor of the exercise by the City of its powers to govern with respect to any matter which is a municipal affair.

Section 701: **Severability**

If any provision of this Charter should be held by a final judgment of a court of competent jurisdiction to be invalid, void or unenforceable, the remaining provisions of this Charter shall remain enforceable to the fullest extent permitted by law.

Article 8: Amendment

Section 800: **Amendment to Charter, Revised or Repealed**

This Charter, and any of its provisions, may be amended by a majority vote of the electors voting on the question. Amendment or repeal may be proposed by initiative or by the governing body.

**The Home Rule Charter of
The City of Cerritos, California**

Table of Contents

Preamble **Page 79**

Article I: **Incorporation and Succession** **Page 80**

Section 100: Name and Boundaries

Section 101: Succession, Rights, and Liabilities

Section 102: Ordinances

Section 103: Continuance of Present Officers and Employees

Section 104: Effective Date of Charter

Article II: **Powers of City** **Page 82**

Section 200: Powers

Article III: **Form of Government** **Page 83**

Section 300: Form of Government

Article IV: **Elective Officers** **Page 84**

Section 400: Elective Officers

Section 401: Eligibility

Section 402: Compensation

Section 403: Vacancies

Section 404:	City Council, Presiding Officer, Mayor	
Section 405:	Powers Vested in the City Council	
Section 406:	Interference in Administrative Service	
Section 407:	Regular Meetings	
Section 408:	Special Meetings	
Section 409:	Place of Meeting	
Section 410:	Quorum, Proceedings	
Section 411:	Citizen Participation	
Section 412:	Adoption of Ordinances and Resolutions	
Section 413:	Ordinances; Publication	
Section 414:	Codification of Ordinances	
Section 415:	Ordinances, When Effective	
Section 416:	Ordinances, Violation, Penalty	
Section 417:	Publishing of Legal Notices	
Article V:	**City Manager**	**Page 93**
Section 500:	City Manager	
Section 501:	City Manager; Powers and Duties	
Section 502:	City Manager; Meetings	

Article VI: **Officers and Employees** **Page 95**

Section 600: Officers to be Appointed by the City Council

Section 601: Administrative Department

Section 602: City Clerk; Powers and Duties

Section 603: Treasurer

Section 604: City Attorney; Powers and Duties

Section 605: Administering Oaths

Section 606: Illegal Contracts, Financial Interest

Section 607: Acceptance of Other Office

Section 608: Official Bonds

Article VII: **Appointive Boards and Commissions** **Page 101**

Section 700: In General

Sections 701, 702, 703, 704 and 705: Repealed

Article VIII: Elections **Page 102**

Section 800: General Municipal Elections

Section 801: Special Municipal Elections

Section 802: Procedure for Holding Elections

Section 803: Initiative, Referendum and Recall

Article IX:	**Fiscal Administration**	**Page 104**

Section 900: Fiscal Year

Section 901: Annual Budget; Preparation by the City Manager

Section 902: Budget, Submission to City Council

Section 903: Tax Limits

Section 904: Bonded Debt Limit

Section 905: Contracts on Public Works

Section 906: Presentation of Demands

Section 907: Registering Warrants

Section 908: Actions Against City-charter

Section 909: Independent Audit

Article X:	**Franchises**	**Page 110**

Section 1000: Granting of Franchises

Section 1001: Resolution of Intention; Notice and Public Hearing'

Section 1002: Term of Franchises

Section 1003: Grant to be in Lieu of All Other Franchises

Section 1004: Eminent Domain

Section 1005:	Duties of Grantees	
Section 1006:	Exercising Rights Without Franchise	
Article XI:	**Miscellaneous**	**Page 115**
Section 1100:	Definitions	
Section 1101:	Purpose of Charter	
Section 1102:	Violations	
Section 1103:	Validity	
Clerk's Certificate		**Page 117**

Preamble

We, the people of the City of Cerritos, State of California, do ordain and establish this Charter as the organic law of the City under the Constitution of the State.

Article I: Incorporation and Succession

Section 100: Name and Boundaries

The name of this City shall be "City of Cerritos" and said City shall continue to be a municipal corporation under such name. Whenever the term "City" or "City of Dairy Valley," the former name of this City, shall appear in this Charter or in any contract, ordinance, resolution, order or other document or action of this City, said term shall refer to and mean the City of Cerritos. The boundaries of the City shall be the boundaries as established at the time the Charter of this City took effect or as such boundaries may have been, or be, changed thereafter in the manner authorized by law.

Section 101: Succession, Rights, and Liabilities

The City of Cerritos shall continue to own, possess, and control all rights and property of every kind and nature owned, possessed, or controlled by it at the time this Charter takes effect and shall be subject to all its debts, obligations, liabilities, and contracts.

Section 102: Ordinances

All lawful ordinances, resolutions, rules and regulations, or portions thereof, in force at the time this Charter takes effect, and not in conflict or inconsistent herewith, are hereby continued in force until the same shall have been duly repealed, amended, changed or superseded by proper authority.

Section 103: **Continuance of Present Officers and Employees**

The present officers and employees shall continue to perform the duties of their respective offices and employments without interruption for the same compensations and under the same conditions until the election or appointment, and qualification of their successors under this Charter and subject to such removal and control as is provided herein and subject to other provisions hereof.

Section 104: **Effective Date of Charter**

This Charter shall take effect upon its approval by the Legislature.

Article II: Powers of City

Section 200: Powers

The City shall have the power to make and enforce all laws and regulations in respect to municipal affairs, subject only to such restrictions and limitations as may be provided in this Charter and in the Constitution of the State of California. It shall also have the power to exercise, or act in pursuant to any and all rights, powers, privileges, or procedures, heretofore or hereafter established, granted, or prescribed by any law of the State, by this Charter, or by other lawful authority, or which a municipal corporation might or could exercise, or act pursuant to, under the Constitution of the State of California. The City shall also have the power to contract with any county, city or other governmental body for the performance of city functions or services by such county, city or other body and the city shall also have the power to transfer any of its functions and any of the functions of an officer, board or commission of the city to an officer, board or commission of the county in which the city is situated. The enumeration of this Charter of a particular power shall not be held to be exclusive of, or any limitation upon, the generality of the foregoing provisions.

Article III: Form of Government

Section 300: Form of Government

The municipal Government established by this charter shall be known as the "Council-Manager" form of government.

Article IV: Elective Officers

Section 400:   Elective Officers

The elective officers of the City shall consist of a City Council of five members elected from the City at large at the times and in the manner provided in this Charter and who shall serve for a term of four years until their respective successors quality.

The members of the City Council in office at the time this Charter takes effect shall continue in office until the expiration of their respective terms.

The term of each elective officer shall commence on the first Wednesday following his election. Ties among candidates for any office shall be settled by the casting of lots.

Limitation of Terms:

This proposed amendment provides that any council member who has served two consecutive four year terms shall not be eligible, for a period of two years, to seek reelection or be appointed to the Cerritos City Council. This amendment will not affect the term of any council member presently in office. This amendment will become effective at the first city council election following its adoption.

Section 401:   Eligibility

No person shall be eligible to hold an elective office unless he is, and shall have been for at least one year immediately preceding his election or appointment, a qualified elector of the City.

Section 402:   Compensation

The members of the City Council shall receive a salary in such amount as the City Council may by ordinance, from time to time approve. The members of the City Council shall receive reimbursement on order of the City Council for council authorized traveling and other expenses when on official duty.

The City Clerk and City Treasurer shall receive compensation for their services in such amount and at such stated times as shall be prescribed by resolution adopted by the City Council.

Section 403:   Vacancies

A vacancy in an elective office, from whatever cause arising, shall be filled by appointment by the City Council, such appointee to hold office for the remainder of such unexpired term and until his successor qualifies.

If a member of the City Council absents himself from all regular meetings of the City Council for a period of sixty days consecutively from and after the last regular City Council meeting attended by such member, unless by permission of the City Council expressed in its official minutes, or is convicted or a crime involving moral turpitude, or ceases to be a qualified elector of the City, his office shall become vacant.

The City Council shall declare the existence of an vacancy. In the event it shall fail to fill a vacancy by appointment within thirty days after such office shall have been declared vacant, it shall cause an election to be held forthwith to fill such vacancy.

Section 404:   City Council, Presiding Officer, Mayor

(A) On the first Wednesday following any general or special municipal election at which any councilman or councilmen is or are elected, the City Council shall meet and shall eclect one of its members as its presiding officer, who shall have the title of Mayor. The Mayor shall have a voice and vote in all its proceedings. He shall be the official head of the City for all ceremonial purposes. The mayor shall also act in a liaison capacity between the City Council and the City Manger, and in such capacity shall advise the City Manager on matters of Council policy. He shall perform such other duties consistent with his office as may be prescribed by this Charter or as may be imposed by the City Council. The Mayor shall serve in such capacity at the pleasure of the City Council.

(B)   Mayor Pro Tempore

The City Council shall also designate one of its members as Mayor Pro Tempore, who shall serve in such capacity at the pleasure of the City Council. The Mayor Pro Tempore shall perform the duties of Mayor during his absence or disability.

Section 405:   Powers Vested in the City Council

All powers of the City shall be vested in the City Council except as otherwise provided in this Charter.

Section 406:   Interference in Administrative Service

Neither the City Council nor any of its members shall interfere with the execution by the City Manager of his powers and duties, or order, directly or indirectly, the appointment by the City Manager or by any of the department heads in the administrative service of the City, of any person to an office or employments or his removal therefrom. Except for the purpose of inquiry, the City Council and its members shall deal with the administrative service under the City Manager solely through the City Manager and neither the City Council nor any member thereof shall give orders to any subordinate of the City Manager, either publicly or privately.

Section 407: Regular Meetings

The City Council shall hold regular meetings at least once each month at such times as it shall fix by ordinance or resolution and may adjourn or re-adjourn any regular meeting to a date and hour certain which shall be specified in the order of adjournment and when so adjourned each adjourned meeting shall be a regular meeting for all presupposes. If the hour to which a meeting is adjourned is not stated in the order of adjournments, such meeting shall be held at the hour for holding regular meetings. If at any time any regular meeting falls on a holiday, such regular meeting shall be held on the next business day.

Section 408: Special Meetings

Special Meetings may be called at any time by the Mayor, or by three members of the City Council, by delivering personally or by mail, written notice to each member of the City Council and to each local newspaper of general circulation, and radio or television station requesting notice in writing. Such notice shall be delivered personally or by mail at least 24 hours before the time of such meetings as specified in the notice. The notice shall specify the business to be transacted and only such matters may be acted upon as are referred to in such written notice. A Special Meeting may be validly held without the giving of such written notice if all members shall give their consent, in writing, to the holding of such meeting and such consent is on file in the Office of the City Clerk at the time of such meeting. Written notice may also be dispensed with as to any member who is actually present at the meeting at the time it convenes. Such waiver may be by telegram.

Section 409: Place of Meeting

All meetings shall be held in such place as the City Council shall fix by ordinance or resolution, or in such place to which any such meeting may be adjourned, and shall be open to the public. If, by reason of fire, flood, or other emergency, it shall be unsafe to meet in the place designated, the meetings will be held for the duration of the emergency at such place as is designated by the Mayor or, if he should fail to act, by three members of the City Council.

Section 410: Quorum, Proceedings

A majority of the members of the City Council shall constitute a quorum to do business but a less number may adjourn from time to time. In the absence of all the members of the City Council from any regular meeting, the City Clerk may declare the same adjourned to a stated day and hour. Notice of a meeting adjourned by less tan a quorum or by the clerk shall be given by the clerk or may be waived by consent in the same manner as specified in this Charter for the giving or waiving of notice of special meetings of the City Council, but need not specify the matters to be acted upon.

The City Council shall judge the qualifications of its members as set forth by the Charter. It shall judge all election returns. It may establish rules for the conduct of its proceedings and evict or prosecute any member or other person for disorderly conduct at any of its meetings.

Each member of the City Council shall have the power to administer oaths and affirmations in any investigation or proceeding pending before the City Council. The City Council shall have the power and authority to compel the attendance of witnesses, to examine them under oath, and to compel the production of evidence before it. Subpoenas shall be issued in the name of the City and attested by the City Clerk. Disobedience of such subpoenas, or the refusal to testify (upon other than constitutional grounds), shall constitute a misdemeanor, or shall be punishable in the same manner as violations of this Charter are punishable.

At the demand of any member or upon the adoption of any ordinance, resolutions, or order for payment of money, the City Clerk shall call the roll and shall cause the ayes and noes taken on such question to be entered upon the minutes of the meeting.

Section 411: **Citizen Participation**

No citizen shall be denied the right, personally or through counsel, to present grievances at any regular meeting of the Council, or offer suggestions for the betterment of municipal affairs.

Section 412: **Adoption of Ordinances and Resolutions**

With the sole exception of ordinances which take effect upon adoption, referred to in this Article, no ordinance shall be adopted by the City Council on the day of its introduction, nor within five days thereafter, nor at any time other than at a regular or adjourned regular meeting. However, an urgency ordinance may be passed immediately upon introduction and either at a regular or special meeting. At the time of its introduction an ordinance shall become part of the proceedings of such meeting in the custody of the City Clerk. At the time of adoption of an ordinance or resolution, it shall be read in full, unless after the reading of the title thereof, the further reading thereof is waved by unanimous consent of the councilmen present. In the event that any ordinance is altered after its introduction, the same shall not be finally adopted except at a regular or adjourned regular meeting held not less than five days after the date upon which such ordinance was altered. The correction of typographical or clerical errors shall not constitute the meaning of an alteration within the meaning of the foregoing sentence.

Unless a different vote is required by other provisions of the Charter, the affirmative votes of at least three members of the City Council shall be required for the enactment of any ordinance or resolution, or for the meaning or approving of any order for the payment of money. All ordinances and resolutions shall be signed by the Mayor and attested by the City Clerk.

Any ordinance declared by the City Council to be necessary as an emergency measure for preserving the public peace, health, or safety, and containing a statement of the reasons for its urgency, may be introduced and adopted at one and the same meeting.

Section 413:   Ordinances; Publication

The City Clerk shall cause each ordinance to be published at least once in the official newspaper, if any, within fifteen days after its adoption.

Section 414:   Codification of Ordinances

Any or all ordinances of the City which have been enacted and published in the manner required at the time of their adoption and which have not been repealed, may be compiled, consolidated, revised, indexed and arranged as a comprehensive ordinance code, and such code may be adopted by reference, with the same effect as an ordinance, bye the passage of an ordinance for such purpose. Such code need not be published in the manner required for other ordinances, but not less than three copes thereof shall be filed for use and examination by public in the office of the City Clerk prior to the adoption thereof. Ordinances codified shall be repealed as the effective date of the code. Amendments to the code shall be enacted in the same manner as ordinances.

Detailed regulations pertaining to the construction of buildings, plumbing, and wiring, when arranged as a comprehensive code, may likewise be adopted by reference in the manner provided in this section.

Section 415: **Ordinances, When Effective**

No ordinance shall be effective until thirty days from and after the date of its adoption, except the following, which shall take effect upon adoption:

(A) An ordinance calling or otherwise relating to an election.

(B) An improvement proceeding ordinance adopted under some law or procedural ordinance.

(C) An ordinance relating to taxes, if any, for the usual and current expenses of the City.

(D) An emergency ordinance adopted in the manner, provided for in this Article.

Section 416: **Ordinances, Violation, Penalty**

A violation of any ordinance of the City shall constitute a misdemeanor and may be prosecuted in the name of the People of the State of California or may be redressed by civil action. The maximum fine or penalty for any violation of a city ordinance shall be the sum of $500.00 or a term of imprisonment not exceeding six months, or both such fine and imprisonment.

Section 417: **Publishing of Legal Notices**

In the event that there is more than one newspaper in circulation published and circulated in the City, the City Council, annually, prior to the beginning of each fiscal year, shall publish a notice inviting bids and contract for the publication of all legal notices or other matter required to be published in a newspaper of general circulation in said City, during the ensuing fiscal year. IN the even there is only one newspaper of general circulation published and circulated in the the City, then the City Council shall have the power to contract with such newspaper for the printing and publishing of such legal notices or mater without being required to advertise for bids thereof. The newspaper with which any such contract is made shall be designate the official newspaper for the publishing of such notices or other matter for the period of such contract.

In no case shall the contract prices for such publication exceed the customary rates charged by such newspaper for the publication of legal notices of private character.

In the even there is no newspaper of general circulation published and circulated in the City, then all legal notices and other matter may be published by posting copies thereof in at least three public places in the City. No defect or irregularity in proceedings taken under this section, or failure to designate an official newspaper, shall invalidate any publication where the same is otherwise in conformity with this Charter or law or ordinance.

Article V: City Manager

Section 500: **City Manager**

There shall be a City Manger who shall be the chief administrative officer of the City. IN the selection of a city manager the City Council shall screen all applicants and other qualified persons known by the council to be available. It shall appoint, by a majority vote, the person that it believes to be the best qualified on the basis of his executive and administrative qualifications, with special referee to his experience in, or his knowledge of, accepted practice in respect to the duties of the office as set forth in this Charter. The City Manger shall serve at the pleasure of the City Council.

No person shall be eligible to receive appointment as City Manager while serving as a member of the City Council nor within one year after he has cased to be councilman.

Section 501: **City Manager; Powers and Duties**

The City Manager shall be the head of the administrative branch of the city government. He shall be responsible to the City Council for the proper administration of all affairs of the City. Without limiting the foregoing general grant of powers, responsibilities and duties, the City Manager shall have power and be required to:

(A) Appoint, suspend, or remove all department heads and officers of the City except officers and those department heads and officers the power of whose appointment is vested by the Charter in City Council.

(B) Prepare the budget annually, submit such budget to the City Council, and be responsible for its administration after its adoption.

(C) Prepare and submit to the City Council as of the end of the fiscal year a comprehensive report on the finances and administrative activities of the City for the preceding year.

(D) Keep the City Council advised of the financial condition and the future needs of the City and make such recommendations as may seem to him desirable.

(E) Prepare rules and regulations governing the contracting for, purchasing, storing, distribution, or disposal of all supplies, materials, and equipment required by any office, department, or agency of the City government and recommend them to the City Council for adoption by it by ordinance.

(F) Perform such other duties consistent with this Charter as may be required of him by the City Council by ordinance or otherwise.

Section 502:   City Manager; Meetings

The City Manger shall be accorded a seat at the City Council table and at all meetings of boards and commissions and shall be entitled to participate in their deliberations, but shall not have a vote.

Article VI: Officers and Employees

Section 600:   Officers to be Appointed by the City Council

In addition to the City Manager, there shall be a City Clerk, City Treasurer, City Attorney, and, in the discretion of the City Council, an Assistant City Attorney, who shall be appointed by and serve at the pleasure of the City Council. The offices of City Clerk and City Treasurer may be held by the same person.

Section 601:   Administrative Department

The City Council may provide by ordinance not inconsistent with this Charter for the organization, conduct, and operation of the several offices and departments of the City as established by this Charter, for the creation of additional departments, divisions, offices, and agencies and for their consolidation, alteration, or abolition. Each new department created by the City Council shall be headed by an officer as department head who shall be appointed and may be suspended or removed by the City Manager.

The City Council, by ordinance or resolution, may assign additional functions or duties to offices, departments, or agencies not inconsistent with this Charter. The City Council shall provide for the number, titles, qualifications, powers, duties, and compensation of all officers and employees.

Section 602:   City Clerk; Powers and Duties

The City Clerk shall have power and be required to:

(A)   Attend all meetings of the City Council and be responsible for the recording and maintaining of a full and true record of all the proceedings of the City Council in books which shall bear appropriate titles and be devoted to such purposes.

(B) Maintain seperate books in which shall be recorded respectively all ordinances and resolutions, with a certificate of the Clerk annexed to each thereof stating the same to be the original or a corrected copy, and as to an ordinance requiring publication, stating that the same has been published or posted in accordance with this Charter; keep all books properly indexed and open to public inspection when not in actual use.

(C) Maintain seperate books in which a record shall be made of all written contracts and fidelity and performance bonds.

(D) Be the custodian of the Seal of the City.

(E) Administer oaths or affirmations, take affidavits and depositions pertaining to the affairs and business of the City, and certify copies of the official records.

(F) Be ex officio assessor, unless the City Council has availed itself or does in the future avail itself of the provisions of the general laws of the State relative to any assessment of property and the collection of city taxes, if any, by county officers, or the City Council by ordinance provides otherwise.

(G) Be responsible for the conduct of all city elections.

(H) Deputize other persons to assist in carrying out the duties of the City Clerk.

Section 603: **Treasurer**

There shall be a treasurer who shall have power and shall be required to:

(A) Collect any license fees or other revenues of the City, or for whose collection the City is responsible and receive all taxes or other money receivable by the City from the County, State or Federal government, or from any Court or from any office, department or agency of the City.

(B) Have custody of all public funds belonging to or under control of the City or any office, department or agency of the City government and deposit all funds coming into his hands in such depository as may be designated by resolution of the City Council or if no such resolution be adopted, then in such depository designated in writing by the City Manager, and in compliance with all of the provisions of the State Constitution and laws of the State governing the handling, depositing and securing of public funds.

(C) Disburse moneys on demands audited in the manner provided for in the Charter.

(D) Prepare and submit to the City Council monthly written reports of all receipts, disbursements and fund balances, copies of which reports shall be filed with the City Manager.

Section 604: **City Attorney; Powers and Duties**

To become eligible for City Attorney or Assistant City Attorney the person appointed shall be an attorney at law licensed as such under the laws of the State of California and shall have engaged in the practice of law for at least two years prior to his appointment. The City Attorney shall have power and be required to:

(A) Represent and advise the City Council and all city officers in matters of law pertaining to their office.

(B) Represent and appear for the City in any or all actions and proceedings in which the City is concerned or is a party, except the prosecution of criminal actions, and represent and appear for any city officer or employee, or former city officer or employee, in any or all actions and proceedings in which any such officer or employee is concerned or is a party, for any act arising out of his employment or by reason by his official capacity.

(C) Attend all regular meetings of the City Council and give his advice and opinions in writing whenever requested to do so by the City Council or by any of the boards or officers of the City.

(D) Approve the form of all contracts made by, and all bonds given to, the City, endorsing his approval thereon in writing.

(E) Prepare any and all proposed ordinances or resolutions for the City and amendments thereto.

(F) Approve, as to legality, all investments of City funds.

The City Council shall have control of all legal business and proceedings and may employ other attorneys to take charge of a litigation or matter or to assist the City Attorney therein.

Section 605: Administering Oaths

Each department head and his deputies shall have the power to administer oaths and affirmations in connection with any official business pertaining to his department.

Section 606: Illegal Contracts, Financial Interest

No member of the City Council, department head or other officer of the City (except a member of any board or commission), shall be financially interested, directly or indirectly in any contract, sale or transaction to which the City is a party.

No member of any board or commission shall be financially interested, directly or indirectly, in any contract, sale or transaction to which the City is a party and which comes before the board or commission of which such person is a member for approval or other official action or which pertains to the department, office or agency of the City with which such board or commission is connected.

Any contract, sale or transaction in which there shall be such an interest, as specified in this section, shall become void at the option of the City when so declared by resolution of the City Council.

No member of the City Council, department head or other officer of the City, or member of any board or commission shall be deemed to be financially interested, within the meaning of the foregoing provisions, in any contract made with a corporation where his only interest in the corporation is that of a stockholder and the stock owned by him shall amount to less than three percent of all the stock of such corporation issued and outstanding.

If any member of the City Council, department head or other officer of the City, or member of a board or commission shall be financially interested as aforesaid, upon conviction thereof he shall forfeit his office in addition to any other penalty which may be imposed for such violation of this Charter.

Section 607: **Acceptance of Other Office**

Any elective officer of the City who shall accept or retain any other elective public office shall be deemed thereby to have vacated his office under the City Government.

Section 608: **Official Bonds**

The City Council shall fix by ordinance or resolution the amounts and terms of the official bonds of all officials or employees who are required by ordinance to give such bonds. All bonds shall be executed by responsible corporate surety, shall be approved as to form by the City Attorney, and shall be filed with the City Clerk. Premiums on official bonds shall be paid by the City.

100

There shall be no personal liability upon, or any right to recover against, a superior officer, or his bond for any wrongful act or omission of his subordinate unless such superior officer was a party to, or conspired in, such wrongful act or omission.

Article VII: Appointive Boards and Commissions

Section 700: In General

Except where specific State law provides the manner in which boards or commissions are to be created, the City Council may create by resolution, such boards or commissions as in its judgement are required and may grant them such power and duties as are consistent with the provisions of this Charter as determined by the City Council.

Sections 701, 702, 703, 704 and 705:

Repealed

Article VIII: Elections

Section 800: General Municipal Elections

General municipal elections for the election of officers and for such other purposes as the City Council may prescribe may be held in the City on any of the dates established by the law of the State of California for general municipal elections in general law cities. The date for the election shall be determined by ordinance of the City Council, which shall remain in effect until amended by a subsequent ordinance. A change in the date of the general municipal election may change the length of a term of office, whether established by this Charter or otherwise, but only to the extent required to accommodate that change of date, and subject to the limitation that as a result of any ordinance effecting a change in date of an election, no term of office shall be increased or decreased by more than 12 months; thereafter, such terms of office shall be of such length as is otherwise provided by law.

Section 801: Special Municipal Elections

All other municipal elections that may be held by authority of this Charter, or of any law, shall be known as special municipal elections.

Section 802: Procedure for Holding Elections

Unless otherwise provided by ordinance hereafter enacted, all elections shall be held in accordance with the provisions of the Elections Code of the State of California, as the same now exist or hereafter may be amended, for the holding of elections in general law cities so far as the same are not in conflict with this Charter.

Section 803: **Initiative, Referendum and Recall**

There are hereby reserved to the electors of the City the powers of the initiative and referendum and of the recall of municipal elective officers. The provisions of the Election Code of the State of California, as the same now exist or hereafter may be amended, governing the initiative and referendum and the recall of municipal officers, shall apply to the use thereof in the City so far as such provisions of the Elections Code are not in conflict with the provisions of this charter.

Article IX: Fiscal Administration

Section 900: Fiscal Year

The fiscal year of the City government shall begin on the first day of July of each year and end on the thirtieth day of June the following year.

Section 901: Annual Budget; Preparation by the City Manager

At such date as he shall determine, the City Manager shall obtain from each department head estimates of revenue and expenditures of his department, detailed in such manner as may be prescribed by the City Manager. In preparing the proposed budget, the City Manager shall review the estimates, hold conferences thereon with the respective department heads and may revise the estimate as he may dem advisable.

Section 902: Budget, Submission to City Council

At least thirty five days prior to the beginning of each fiscal year, the City Manager shall submit to the City Council the proposed budget as prepared by him. Copies of the proposed budget shall be available for inspection by the public in the office of the City Clerk. At a regular meeting, the City Council shall consider the proposed budget and make any revisions thereof that it may deem advisable and on or before August 31, it shall adopt the budget. A copy thereof, certified by the City Clerk, shall be filed with the person retained by the City Council to perform auditing functions for the Council and a further copy shall be placed and shall remain on file in the office of the City Clerk where it shall be available for inspection.

Section 903: Tax Limits

(A) In the event the City Council shall ever determine that it is necessary to levy a property tax for municipal purposes, any such tax shall not be in excess of One Dollar annually for each One Hundred Dollars of the assessed value of taxable property in the City, except as otherwise provided in this section, unless authorized by the affirmative votes for two-thirds of the electors voting on a proposition to increase such levy at any election at which the question of such additional levy for municipal purposes is submitted to the electors. The number of years that such additional levy is to be made shall be specified in such proposition.

(B) The City Council shall be empowered to levy and collect at the time and in the same manner as other property taxes, if any, for municipal purposes are levied and collected, as additional taxes, if no other provision for payment thereof is made.

(C) A tax sufficient to meet all liabilities of the City for principal and interest of all bonds or judgments due and unpaid, or to become due during the ensuing fiscal year, which constitute general obligations of the City.

(D) The procedure for the assessment, levy, and collection of taxes, if ever, upon property, taxable for municipal purposes may be prescribed by ordinance of the City Council.

Section 904: Bonded Debt Limit

The City shall not incur an indebtedness evidenced by general obligation bonds which shall in the aggregate exceed the sum of fifteen percent of the total assessed valuation, for purposes of city taxation, of all the real and personal property within the City, exclusive of any indebtedness that may hereafter be incurred for the purpose of constructing sewers or drains in the City, for which purposes a further indebtedness may be incurred for the issuance of bonds, subject only to the provisions of the State Constitution and of this Charter.

No bonded indebtedness which shall constitute a general obligation of the City may be created unless authorized by the affirmative votes of two-thirds of the electors voting on such proposition at any election at which the question is submitted to the electors and unless in full compliance with the provisos of the State Constitution and this Charter.

Section 905:   Contracts on Public Works

Every project involving an expenditure of more than Seven Thousand Five Hundred ?Dollars for the construction or improvement of public buildings, works, streets, drains, sewers, utilities, parks or playgrounds shall be let by the City Council by contract to the lowest responsible bidder after notice by publication in the official newspaper by one or more insertions, the first of which shall be at least ten days before the time for opening bids. Projects for the construction, resurfacing, maintenance or repair of street, drains or sewers are excepted from the requirements of this paragraph if such work is performed by a City or County of Los Angeles department.

All bids shall be accompanied by either a certified or cashier's check, or a bidder's bond executed by a corporate surety authorized to engage in such business in California, made payable to the City. Such security shall be in an amount not less than that specified in the notice inviting bids or in the specifications referred to therein, or if no amount be so specified then in an amount not less than ten percent of the aggregate amount of the bid. If the successful bidder neglects or refuses to enter into the contract, within the time specified in the notice inviting bids or in the specifications referred to therein, the amount of the bidder's security shall be declared forfeited to the City and shall be collected and paid into its general fund, and all bonds so forfeited shall be prosecuted and the amount thereof collected and paid into such fund.

The City Council may reject any and all bids presented and may re-advertise in its discretion.

The City Council, after rejecting bids, or if no bids are received, may declare and determine that in its opinion, baed on estimates approved by the City Manager, the work in question may be performed better or more economically by the City with its own employees or the materials may be purchased more economically on the open market, and after the adoption of a resolution to this effect by at least three affirmative votes of the ?Council may proceed to have said work done in the manner stated, without further observance of the provisions of this section. Such contracts likewise may be let without advertising for bids, if such work shall be deemed by the City Council to be of urgent necessity for the preservation of life, health or property, and shall be authorized by resolution passed by at least three affirmative votes of the Council and containing a declaration of the facts constituting such urgency.

Section 906:   Presentation of Demands

Any demand against the City must be in writing and may be in the form of a bill, invoice, pay roll, or formal demand. Each such demand shall be presented to the City Clerk, who shall examine the same. If the amount thereof is legally due and there remains on his books an un-exhausted balance of an appropriation against which the same me be charged, he shall approve such demand and draw a warrant on the City Treasurer therefor, payable out of the proper fund. Objections of the City clerk may be overruled by the VG and the warrant ordered drawn.

The City Clerk shall transmit such demand, with his approval or rejection thereof, endorsed thereon, and warrant, if any, to the City Manager. If a demand is one for an item included within an approved budget appropriation, it shall require the approval of the City Manager, otherwise it shall require the approval of the City Council. Any person dissatisfied with the refusal of the City Manager to approve any demand, in whole or in part, may present the same to the City Council which, after examining into the matter, may approve or disapprove the demand in whole or in part.

Section 907: **Registering Warrants**

Warrants on the City Treasurer which are not paid for lack of funds shall be registered. All registered warrants shall be paid in the order of their registration when funds therefor are available and shall bear interest from the date of registration at such rate as shall be fixed by the City Council by resolution.

Section 908: **Actions Against City-charter**

No suit shall be brought on any claim for money or damages against the City or any board or officer thereof until a demand for the same had been presented as herein provided and rejected in whole or in part. If rejected in part, suit may be brought to recover the whole. Except in those cases where a shorter time is otherwise provided by law, all claims for damages against the City must be verified and presented to the City Clerk withing the time provided by law, and shall set forth in detail the name and address of the claimant, the time, date place and circumstances o the occurrence and the extent of the injuries or damages received; all other claims or demands shall be presented within ninety days after the last time of the account or claim occurred.

In all cases such claims shall be approved or rejected in writing by order of the City Council and the date thereof given. Failure to complete the action or demand within sixty days from the day the same is filed with the City Clerk shall be deemed a rejection thereof.

Section 909:   Independent Audit

The City Council shall employ at the beginning of each fiscal year, a certified public accountant who shall, at such time or times as may be specified by the City Council, and at such other times as he shall determine, examine the official books, records, inventories and reports of all officers and employees who receive handle or disburse public funds and all such other officers, employees or departments as the City Council may direct. Within sixty days from the end of the fiscal year, unless such time shall be extended by the Council, a final audit and report shall be submitted by such accountant to the City Council, one copy thereof to be distributed to each member, one to the City Manager, Treasurer and City Attorney, respectively, and three additional copes to be placed on file in the office of the City Clerk where they shall be available for inspection by the general public.

Article X: Franchises

Section 1000: Granting of Franchises

Any person, firm or corporation furnishing the City or its inhabitants with transportation, communication, terminal facilities, water, light, heat, gas, power, refrigeration, storage or any other public utility or service, or using the public streets, ways, alleys, or places for operation of plants, works, or equipment for the furnishing thereof or traversing any portion of the City ,for the transmitting or conveying of any such service elsewhere, may be required by ordinance to have a valid and existing franchise thereof. The City Council is empowered to grant such franchise to any person, firm or corporation, whether operating under an existing franchise or not. The City Council may prescribe the terms and conditions of any such grant. It may also provide by procedural ordinance the method of procedure and additional terms and conditions of such grants, or the making thereof, subject to the provisions of this Charter.

Nothing in this Section, or elsewhere in this Article, shall apply to the City, or any department thereof, when furnishing any such utility or service.

Section 1001: Resolution of Intention; Notice and Public Hearing'

Before granting any franchise, the City Council shall pass a resolution declaring its intention to grant the same, stating the name of the proposed grantee, the character of the franchise and the terms and conditions upon which it is proposed to be granted. Such resolution shall fix and set forth the day, hour and place when and where any persons having any interest therein or any objection to the granting thereof may appear before the City Council and be heard thereon. It shall direct the City Clerk to publish, at the expense of the proposed grantee, said resolution at least once within fifteen days of the passage thereof, in the official newspaper. Said notices shall be published at least ten days prior to the date of hearing.

At the time set for the hearing the City Council shall proceed to hear and pass upon all protests and its decision thereon shall be final and conclusive. Thereafter it may grant or deny the franchise on the terms and conditions specified in the resolution of intention to grant the same, subject to the right of referendum of the people. If the City Council shall determine that changes should be made in the terms and conditions upon which the franchise is proposed to be granted, a new resolution of intention shall be adopted and like proceedings had thereon.

Section 1002: **Term of Franchises**

Every franchise, other than an indeterminate franchise, shall state the term for which it is granted, which shall not exceed twenty-five years.

A franchise grant may be indeterminate, that is to say, it may provide that it shall endure in full force and effect until the same, with the consent of the Public Utilities Commission of the State of California, shall be voluntarily surrendered or abandoned by its possessor, or until the State of California or some municipal or public corporation, thereunto duly authorized by law shall purchase or shall condemn and take under the power of eminent domain, all property actually used and useful in the exercise of such franchise and situate within the territorial limits of the State, municipal or public corporation purchasing or condemning such property, or until the franchise shall be forfeited for non-compliance with its terms by the possessor thereof.

Section 1003: **Grant to be in Lieu of All Other Franchises**

Any franchise granted by the City hereunder with respect to any given utility service shall be in lieu of all other franchises, rights or privileges owned by the grantee, or by any successor of the grantee to any rights under such franchise granted hereunder, for the rendering of such utility service within the limits of the City as they now or may hereafter exist except any franchise derived under Section 19 of Article XI of the Constitution of California as said section existed prior to the amendment thereof adopted October 10, 1911. The acceptance of any franchise hereunder shall operate as an abandonment of all such other franchises, rights and privileges within the limits of the City as such limits shall at any time exist.

Any franchise granted hereunder shall not become effective until written acceptance thereof shall have been filed by the grantee thereof with the City Clerk. Such acceptance shall be filed within ten days after the adoption of the ordinance granting the franchise, or any extension thereof granted by the City Council, and when so filed such acceptance shall constitute a continuing agreement of such grantee that if and when the City shall thereafter annex, or consolidate with additional territory, any and all franchises, rights and privileges owned by the grantee therein, except a franchise derived under said constitutional provision, shall likewise be deemed to be abandoned within the limits of such additional territory. No grant of any franchise may be transferred or assigned by the grantee except by consent in writing of the City Council and unless the transferee or assignee thereof shall covenant and agree to perform and be bound by each and all the terms and conditions imposed in the g rant or by procedural ordinance and by this Charter.

Section 1004: Eminent Domain

No franchise grant shall in any way, or to any extent, impair or affect the rights of the City to acquire the property of the grantee thereof either by purchase or through the exercise of the right of eminent domain, and nothing therein contained shall be construed to contract away or to modify or to abridge, either for a term or in perpetuity, the City's right of eminent domain with respect to any public utility.

Section 1005: **Duties of Grantees**

By its acceptance of any franchise hereunder, the grantee shall covenant and agree to perform and be bound by each and all the terms and conditions imposed in the grant or by procedural ordinance and shall further agree to:

(A) Comply with all lawful ordinances, rules and regulations theretofore adopted by the City Council in the exercise of its authority governing the construction, maintenance and operation of its plants, work or equipment.

(B) Pay to the City on demand the cost of all repairs to public property made necessary by any of the operations of the grantee under such franchise.

(C) Indemnify and hold harmless the City and its officers from any and all liabilities for damages proximately resulting from any operations under such franchise.

(D) Remove and relocate without expense to the City any facilities installed, used and maintained under the franchise if and when made necessary by any lawful change of grade, alignment or width of any public street, way, alley or place, including the construction of any subway or viaduct, or if the public health, comfort, welfare, convenience or safety so demands.

(E) Pay the City during the life of the franchise a percentage, to be specified in the grant, of the gross annual receipts of the grantee within the limits of the City, or such other compensation as the City Council may prescribe in the grant.

Section 1006: **Exercising Rights Without Franchise**

The exercise by any person, firm or corporation of any privilege for which a franchise is required, without possessing a valid and existing franchise therefor, shall be a misdemeanor and shall be punishable in the same manner as violations of this Charter are punishable and each day that such condition continues to exist shall constitute a seperate violation.

Article XI: Miscellaneous

Section 1100: **Definitions**

Unless the provision or the context otherwise requires, as used in this Charter:

(A) "Shall" is mandatory and "may" is permissive.

(B) "City" is the City of Cerritos, and "department," "board," "commission," "agency," "officer," or "employee," is a department, board, commission, agency, officer or employee, as the case may be, of the City of Cerritos.

(C) "County" is the County of Los Angeles.

(D) "State" is the State of California.

Section 1101: **Purpose of Charter**

It shall be the purpose of this Charter to maintain a city government responsive to the citizens of the City of Cerritos, to provide adequate local government with a minimum of taxation and, in addition to other municipal purposes, to promote foster and preserve agriculture within the City.

Section 1102: **Violations**

The violation of any provision of this Charter shall be deemed a misdemeanor and be punishable upon conviction by a fine of not exceeding Five Hundred Dollars or by imprisonment for a term of not exceeding six onths or by both such fine and imprisonment.

Section 1103: **Validity**

If any provision of this Charter, or the application thereof to any person or circumstance is held invalid, the remainder of the Charter, and the application of such provision to other persons or circumstances shall not be affected thereby.

Clerk's Certificate

Whereas, the City of Dairy Valley has been and now is a city containing more than three thousand five hundred (3500) inhabitants, as ascertained by the last preceding census taken under the authority of the Congress of the United States or of the Legislature of the State of California, and

Whereas, pursuant to the provisions of Section 8 of Article XI of the Constitution of the State of California, the City Council of the City of Dairy Valley, being the legislative body thereof, on its own motion did cause to be framed the foregoing Charter as a proposed Charter for the City of Dairy Valley and did cause the same to be filed in the office of the City Clerk of the City of Dairy Valley on December 22, 1958.

BE IT KNOWN, that in pursuance of the provisions of said Constitution and pursuant to Resolution No. 138 of the City Council of the City of Dairy Valley, the foregoing proposed Charter was filed in the office of the City Clerk of the City of Dairy Valley on December 22, 1958

DATED December 22, 1958

Attest: Agnes Hickey
City Clerk of the City of Dairy Valley

**The Home Rule Charter of
The City Of Chico, California**

Table of Contents

Preamble   **Page 127**

        Article I: **Incorporation and Succession**   **Page 128**

Section 100:   Name of City

Section 101:   Definition of "city"

Section 102:   Boundaries

Section 103:   Rights and Liabilities

Section 104:   Continuance of Vested Rights

Section 105:   Continuance of Ordinances and Resolutions

Section 106:   Continuance of Present Council Members, Officers and Employees

        Article II: **Powers of the City**   **Page 130**

Section 200:   Legislative Power of the City

Section 201:   General Powers

        Article III: **Form of Government**   **Page 131**

Section 300:   Council-Manager Form of Government

Article IV:	**Elective Officers**	**Page 132**
Section 400:	Enumeration	
Section 401:	Terms Generally	
Section 402:	Elected At Large	
Section 403:	Eligibility of Candidates	
Section 404:	Repealed	
Section 405:	Same; Forfeiture of Office for Failure to Attend Meetings or Conviction of Certain Crimes, Etc.	
Section 406:	Vacancies	
Section 407:	Repealed	
Section 408:	Repealed	
Section 409:	Oath of Office	
Article V:	**Elections**	**Page 136**
Section 500:	General Municipal Elections	
Section 501:	Special Municipal Elections	
Section 502:	Procedure For Holding Elections	
Section 503:	Initiative, Referendum And Recall	
Section 504:	Repealed	

Article VI:	**The Council**	**Page 137**
Section 600:	Membership	
Section 601:	Remuneration	
Section 602:	Meetings	
Section 603:	Mayor, Vice-Mayor, Mayor Pro Tempore	
Section 604:	Powers of the Council	
Section 605:	Appointment of Officers and Commission Members	
Section 606:	Power of Subpoena; Failure to Obey Subpoena	
Section 607:	Rules of Procedure	
Section 608:	Council Members Ineligible to Other City Positions	
Section 609:	Ordinances and Resolutions Generally	
Section 610:	Ordinance; Title and Enacting Clause	
Section 611:	Same; Adoption and Publication	
Section 612:	Same; Emergency Ordinances	
Section 613:	Same; Amendment	
Section 614:	Same; Sale, Exchange, Lease or Purchase of Real Property	

Section 615:	Same; Attesting
Section 616:	Same; Effective Date
Section 617:	Same; Codification and Adoption by Reference
Article VII:	**The City Manager Page 146**
Section 700:	Qualification
Section 701:	Duties and Authority Generally
Article VIII:	**Executive and Administrative Organizations Page 148**
Section 800:	Establishment by Ordinance
Article IX:	**Appointive Officers and Employees Page 149**
Section 900:	Enumerated
Section 901:	Residence Requirements
Section 902:	Oath of Office
Section 903:	Official Bonds
Section 904:	Duties to be Established by Ordinance; Combining Departments or Offices; Suspending or Abolishing Offices
Section 905:	Powers and Duties of City Clerk
Section 906:	Qualifications, Powers and Duties of City Attorney

Section 906.1:	Repealed
Section 907:	Repealed
Section 908:	Finance Director
Section 909:	Compensation of Officers, Department Heads and Employees
Section 910:	Repealed
Section 911:	Nepotism
Section 912:	Delivery of Books, Papers, Etc., to Successors
Section 913:	Inspection of Books and Records
Section 914:	Copies From Books or Records
Article X:	**Appointive Boards and Commissions** **Page 155**
Section 1000:	Generally
Section 1000.1:	Number of Members
Section 1001:	Appointments; Terms
Section 1002:	Repealed
Section 1003:	Organization
Section 1004:	Compensation
Section 1005:	Vacancies

Section 1006:	Bidwell Park and Playground Commission; Creation and Appointment of Members; Suspension
Section 1006.1:	Same; Powers and Duties
Section 1006.2:	Same; Acceptance and Disposition of Donations, Legacies or Bequests
Section 1007:	Airport Commission; Generally; Appointment of Members
Section 1007.1:	Same; Powers and Duties
Section 1008:	Repealed
Section 1008.1:	Repealed
Section 1008.2:	Repealed
Section 1008.3:	Repealed
Section 1008.4:	Repealed
Section 1009:	Repealed
Section 1009.1:	Repealed
Article XI:	**Fiscal Administration** **Page 163**
Section 1100:	The Fiscal Year
Section 1101:	Tax System
Section 1102:	Annual or Biennial Budget

Section 1103:	Budget; Adoption; Fixing of Tax Rates and Assessments	
Section 1104:	Funds	
Section 1105:	Repealed	
Section 1106:	Special Taxes	
Section 1107:	Revenue Bonds	
Section 1108:	Limitation on Bonded Indebtedness	
Section 1109:	Independent Audit	
Section 1110:	Public Works Contracts	
Section 1111:	Form of Contract	
Section 1112:	Regulation of Public Works Contracts	
Section 1113:	Centralized Purchasing	
Section 1114:	Contracts for Legal Publications	
Section 1115:	Claims, Demands and Actions	
Article XII:	**Franchises**	**Page 170**
Section 1200:	Granting of Franchises	
Article XIII:	Repealed	**Page 171**
Article XIV:	**Personnel System**	**Page 172**
Section 1400:	Establishment by Ordinance	

Article XV: Miscellaneous **Page 173**

Section 1500: Definitions

Section 1501: Powers Relative to Streams and Channels

Section 1502: Effective Date of Charter

Section 1503: Severability of Provisions of Charter

Section 1504: Applicability of General Laws of State to City

Section 1505: Violations; Penalties

Preamble

We, the people of the City of Chico, State of California, do ordain and establish this Charter as the organic law of said city under the Constitution of said state.

Article I: Incorporation and Succession

Section 100: Name of City

The municipal corporation now existing in the County of Butte, State of California, and known as the City of Chico shall remain and continue a body politic and corporate in name and in fact by the name of the City of Chico.

Section 101: Definition of "City"

Whenever in this Charter the word "city" occurs, it means the City of Chico; and every "department," "board," "commission," "agency," "officer," or "employee," whenever either is mentioned, means a department, board, commission, agency, officer or employee of the City of Chico.

Section 102: Boundaries

The boundaries of the city shall continue as now established until changed in the manner authorized by law.

Section 103: Rights and Liabilities

The city shall remain vested with, and continue to have, hold, and enjoy all property, rights of property and rights of action of every nature and description now pertaining to this municipality, and is hereby declared to be the successor of the same. It shall be subject to all the liabilities that now exist against this municipality.

Section 104: Continuance of Vested Rights

All vested rights of the city shall continue and shall not in any manner be affected by the adoption of this Charter, nor shall any right, liability, pending suit or prosecution, either in behalf of or against the city, be affected by the adoption of this Charter, unless otherwise herein expressly provided. All contracts entered into by the city or for its benefit prior to the taking effect of this Charter shall be continued and perfected hereunder. Public improvements, for which legislative steps have been taken under laws in force at the time this Charter takes effect, may be carried to completion in accordance with the provisions of such laws.

Section 105: **Continuance of Ordinances and Resolutions**

All ordinances and resolutions in force at the time this Charter takes effect, and not inconsistent therewith, shall continue in full force until amended or repealed.

Section 106: **Continuance of Present Council Members, Officers and Employees**

All council members, officers and employees, when this Charter takes effect, shall continue to hold and exercise their respective offices or employment under the terms of this Charter until the election or appointment and qualification of their successors.

Article II: Powers of the City

Section 200: **Legislative Power of the city**

The legislative power of the city shall be vested in a body to be designated as the council, and in the people through the initiative and the referendum.

Section 201: **General Powers**

The city shall have the power to make and enforce all laws and regulations in respect to municipal affairs, subject only to such restrictions and limitations as may be provided in the Constitution of the State of California, or provision of this Charter. The enumeration in this Charter of any particular power shall not be held to be exclusive of, or any limitation upon, any general power of the city.

Article III: Form of Government

Section 300: **Council-Manager form of Government**

The municipal government provided by this Charter shall be known as the "council- manager" form of government.

Article IV: Elective Officers

Section 400: **Enumeration**

The elective officers of the city shall be seven council members.

Section 401: **Terms Generally**

(A) Council members shall be elected to office at each general municipal election held in the manner hereinafter provided by this Charter. Upon election, council members shall assume office at 7:30 p.m. on the first Tuesday in December following the date of their election and shall hold office for a term of four years thereafter and until successors are elected and qualified.

(B) If, on the date an incoming councilmember is to assume office, the identity of the person elected to such office has not been finally determined, then no person shall be deemed qualified to assume such office until the first meeting held by the council following the date the identity of the person elected to such office has been finally determined and if, on the date an incoming councilmember is to assume office, there is any uncertainty as to which outgoing councilmember has been succeeded, then such uncertainty shall be resolved by the remainder of the council at its meeting on such date.

(C) **Term Limits**

    (I) A person is ineligible to hold office as a member of the city council if that person has served as a member of the city council, including any services as mayor, vice-mayor, or mayor pro tempore, for three (3) consecutive full terms. Nothing in this section shall act to bar any person from serving as a member of the city council after at least two (2) years have elapsed from the person's last full term as a member of the city council.

(II) For the purpose of the term limits set forth in this section, a person who was appointed or elected to a vacant city council position for an unexpired term of more than one-half the original term shall be deemed to have served a full term. Any person who resigns or is removed from office during a term shall be deemed to have served a full term.

(III) The term limits established by this section shall apply prospectively, to those terms of office which commence on or after November 6, 2018. Only those terms of office commencing on or after November 6, 2018 shall be counted towards the term limit established by this Subsection 401.C.

Section 402: **Elected at Large**

Council members of the city shall be elected at large at the general municipal elections provided for in Article V, Section 500, of this charter.

Section 403: **Eligibility of Candidates**

Candidates for city councilmember shall have all of the following qualifications at the time nomination papers are issued:

(A) reside in the city, such residency having been for such period of time, if any, provided by state law for general law cities;

(B) be over the age of twenty-one (21) years; and

(C) be a qualified voter as defined by the Elections Code of the State of California.

Section 404: Repealed

Section 405: **Same; Forfeiture of Office for Failure to Attend Meetings or Conviction of Certain Crimes, Etc.**

If a member of the city council is absent three (3) consecutive regular meetings, such member shall forfeit such member's office unless excused by the council for cause and so recorded in its official minutes. If a member of the city council is adjudged legally incompetent, or ceases to be an elector of the city, or is convicted of a crime involving moral turpitude, such member's office shall become vacant and shall be so declared by the council.

Section 406: **Vacancies**

(A) Any vacancy in the office of councilmember shall be filled for the remainder of the unexpired term by special election called by the council to elect a successor and to be held as soon as practicable. However, a special election need not be called if

(1) the term of the vacant office ends less than six months from the date the vacancy occurred or, when a declaration of vacancy by the council is necessary to establish the vacancy, the effective date of the vacancy so declared, and

(2) the election cannot be held earlier than the 42nd day before the next general municipal election for election of council members.

(B) Notwithstanding subsection A, during the first 30 days of any vacancy, the council may, in lieu of calling a special election, fill the vacancy by appointment of a person qualified to be a candidate for city councilmember. The appointee shall hold office until the first Tuesday in December following the next general municipal election and until the appointee's successor qualifies.

At the next general municipal election following any such appointment, a successor shall be elected to serve for the remainder of any unexpired term.

Section 407: Repealed

Section 408: Repealed

Section 409: **Oath of Office**

An elective officer of the city, before entering upon the duties of the office to which such officer was elected, shall take the oath of office as provided for in the Constitution of the State of California and shall file the same with the city clerk.

Article V: Elections

Section 500: General Municipal Elections

General municipal elections for the election of council members of the city, and for such other purposes as the council may prescribe, shall be held in the city on the first Tuesday after the first Monday in November of each even-numbered year.

Section 501: Special Municipal Elections

All other municipal elections may be held by authority of general law, or by ordinance, and shall be known as special municipal elections. The city council may determine that any special municipal election shall be held by mailed ballot notwithstanding any provision of the general law to the contrary.

Section 502: Procedure for Holding Elections

Unless otherwise provided by ordinance, all elections shall be held in accordance with the provisions of the California Elections Code applicable to elections in general law cities, insofar as the same are not in conflict with this Charter.

The council shall, by ordinance or resolution, order the calling and holding of elections within the city

Section 503: Initiative, Referendum and Recall

The provisions of the Election Code of the State of California 1 governing the initiative, the referendum and the recall of municipal officers shall apply to the use thereof in the city.

Section 504: Repealed

Article VI: The Council

Section 600: **Membership**

The council shall consist of seven (7) council members elected from the city at large in the manner provided for in Article IV, Elective Officers.

Section 601: **Remuneration**

(A) Each councilmember shall receive the maximum monthly salary allowed for councilmembers in general law cities on the salary schedule set forth in California Government Code section 36516(a), as that schedule now exists or may hereafter be amended. This salary shall be adjusted pursuant to that schedule whenever the official population of the city increases or decreases, as determined by the latest decennial federal census, a subsequent census, or the state Department of Finance. The mayor shall receive, in addition to this remuneration as a councilmember, a monthly salary equal to twenty percent (20%) of the monthly salary of a councilmember. Each councilmember, including the mayor, may also be reimbursed for reasonable and necessary expenses actually incurred in the service of the city, provided that an appropriation for such expenses has been made in the budget adopted by the council as provided by this Charter.

(B) Notwithstanding subsection A, an ordinance approved by a majority of the voters voting on the measure may adjust the salary for the office of councilmember or mayor or both offices, to take effect at the commencement of the next term of office or such later time as the ordinance may provide.

Section 602: Meetings

(A) The council shall meet in regular session at 7:30 p.m. on the first Tuesday of each month, provided, however, that the council may designate a different time and date by ordinance subject to the following conditions: (1) such ordinance shall provide for meetings no less often than once each month; and (2) such ordinance shall provide for a regular meeting at 6:00 p.m. of the first Tuesday in December of each even-numbered year.

(B) The council may meet at such other times as it shall determine. A special meeting may be called by the mayor, or any four (4) members. Written notice of such special meeting and the purposes thereof shall be given to each member of the council not less than twenty-four (24) hours before the meeting or within that time prescribed by state law, whichever is greater. At any special meeting, only such matters may be acted upon as are referred to in the said written notice or consent. All meetings shall be held in the council chamber building of the city unless another location is designated by ordinance, or in such a place to which any such meeting may be adjourned.

Section 603: Mayor, Vice-Mayor, Mayor Pro Tempore

(A) The mayor and vice-mayor shall be chosen by the council at its first meeting in December in each even-numbered year to serve for a term of two (2) years. Should a vacancy occur in either the office of mayor or vice-mayor, the council shall elect a successor to serve for the remainder of the unexpired term.

(B) The mayor shall preside over the sessions of the council and shall sign official documents when the signature of the mayor is required by law. The mayor shall be recognized as the official head of the city for all public and ceremonial purposes, and by the Governor for military purposes. In times of emergency, the mayor may take command of the police, maintain order and enforce laws for a period not exceeding forty-eight (48) hours, and the mayor shall be the judge of what constitutes such public dangers or emergencies; such command may be continued for a longer period by a majority of the city council at a special meeting called for that purpose. The mayor shall exercise such other powers and perform such other duties as may be prescribed by law or ordinance or by resolution of the council, except as limited by this Charter. The mayor shall possess no veto power.

(C) The vice-mayor shall, in the absence of the mayor, assume all his or her powers and duties.

(D) When both the mayor and vice-mayor are absent, the council may choose one of its own members to act as mayor pro tempore.

Section 604: **Powers of Council**

Subject to the provisions and restrictions of this Charter and of the Constitution of the State of California, the council shall have the power in the name of the city to perform any and all acts appropriate to a municipal corporation.

Section 605: **Appointment of Officers and Commission Members**

The Council shall have the power and authority to appoint a city manager, a city attorney, city clerk and the members of the various boards and commissions. All other officers and department heads shall be appointed by the city manager, subject to confirmation by the council; except that the park director shall be appointed by the city manager subject to confirmation by both the council and the Bidwell Park and Playground commission, the airport manager shall be appointed by the city manager subject to confirmation by both the council and the airport commission, and any assistant city attorney or deputy city attorney shall be appointed by the city attorney subject to confirmation by the council.

Section 606: Power of Subpoena; Failure to Obey Subpoena

The council shall have the power and authority to compel attendance of witnesses, to examine them under oath, and to compel the production of evidence before it. Subpoenas may be issued in the name of the city and be attested to by the city clerk. Disobedience of such subpoenas or the refusal to testify, other than upon constitutional grounds, shall constitute a misdemeanor.

Section 607: Rules of Procedure

The council shall determine its own rules and order of business, subject, but not limited to, the following provisions:

(A) There shall be a Journal of Proceedings of all council meetings which shall be open to the public, except as otherwise provided by law.

(B) The ayes and noes shall be taken upon the passage of all ordinances and resolutions and entered upon the Journal of Proceedings of the council. Upon the request of any member, the ayes and noes shall be taken and recorded on any vote.

(C) A majority of the council shall constitute a quorum for the transaction of business, but a less number may adjourn from time to time and postpone the consideration of pending business.

(D) The council shall appoint such standing and other committees as it may deem necessary.

Section 608: **Council Members Ineligible to Other City Positions**

(A) No councilmember shall

    (1) Be appointed to any board or commission provided for in this Charter except as designated in the Charter or state law;

    (2) Hold any other municipal office; or

    (3) Hold any city employment for compensation paid out of public moneys belonging to or under the control of the city.

(B) Upon expiration of the last term of a councilmember and for a period of 12 months thereafter, the former council member may not be elected or appointed to any office created, or the compensation of which was increased, by the council while the former member served on the council.

Section 609: **Ordinances and Resolutions Generally**

Legislative action shall be taken by the council only by means of an ordinance or resolution. Unless otherwise specified in this Charter ordinances and resolutions shall be adopted upon receiving the affirmative votes of a majority of a quorum of the council present at any regular meeting.

Section 610: **Ordinance; Title and Enacting Clause**

The title of an ordinance shall be sufficient if it refers to the general subject matter of the provisions being enacted, amended or repealed, or to the general purpose of the ordinance, and it need not refer to the specific provisions affected or otherwise delineate or describe the particular additions, deletions or changes made by said ordinance. No ordinances shall be ineffective or void by reason of any defect in the title thereof. The introductory reading of said title shall constitute notice of all of the provisions of said ordinance set out in the copy of said ordinance maintained in the office of the city clerk.

The enacting clause of every ordinance passed by the council shall be: "Be it ordained by the Council of the City of Chico." Ordinances initiated by the people shall have an enacting clause: "Be it ordained by the People of the City of Chico."

Section 611:   Same; Adoption and Publication

(A) No ordinance, other than an emergency ordinance, shall be adopted by the council within five days after its introduction, nor at other than a regular or an adjourned regular meeting. At the time of introduction, an ordinance shall become a part of the proceedings of said meeting in the custody of the city clerk's office available for inspection and review by all interested persons during regular business hours and until such time as said ordinance is adopted and inserted in the records of the city for adopted ordinances as provided in this Charter. The city clerk need not so maintain a copy of any ordinance not adopted within six months of its introduction. No ordinance may be adopted more than six months after its introduction unless the same is again introduced as hereinabove provided. An ordinance may be introduced and adopted by the reading of the title only, provided that upon the request of any councilmember, and with the consent of a majority of the council present, an ordinance shall be read in full.

(B) An ordinance altered or amended after its introduction and before adoption shall be re-introduced and shall not be adopted within five (5) days of its re-introduction. Corrections of typographical errors or clerical errors which do not change the intent expressed in the ordinance shall not be deemed alterations or amendments within the meaning of this subsection.

(C) Every ordinance must be published in full or in summary, as authorized by State law; once in the official newspaper of the city, or in such other form as it may be sent to the voters. One copy of every ordinance introduced shall be posted by the clerk within twenty-four hours after introductory reading on the public bulletin board in the municipal building of the city, and another copy thereof shall be available in the council chambers during each meeting at which said ordinance is considered by the council for review by all persons interested therein.

Section 612: Same; Emergency Ordinances

Any ordinance declared by the council to be necessary as an emergency measure for preserving the public peace, welfare, health or safety, and containing a statement of the reasons for its urgency, may be introduced by reading in full, and adopted at the same meeting if passed by at least four (4) affirmative votes. No such emergency ordinance shall remain in effect for a period longer than six (6) months. The city council may also adopt an interim zoning ordinance as an emergency measure provided such interim zoning ordinance is adopted in the manner provided by state law.

Section 613: Same; Amendment

No ordinance shall be revised, reenacted or amended by reference to its title only; but the ordinance may be revised or reenacted, or the section, sections, or subsections thereof to be amended, or the new section, sections, or subsections to be added thereto shall be set forth at length as to the particular section, sections, or subsection to be so revised, reenacted or adopted and adopted in the method provided in Section 611 of this Charter. No ordinance or section or subsection thereof shall be repealed except by an ordinance adopted in the manner provided in this Charter, provided that an ordinance, section or subsection thereof may be repealed by reference to the number of the ordinance, section or subsection and to the title of the ordinance or section.

Section 614: Same; Sale, Exchange, Lease or Purchase of Real Property

The sale or exchange of real property owned by the city shall be authorized by resolution adopted by the affirmative vote of at least five (5) members of the council, provided that this section shall not apply to properties dedicated to the City of Chico for park purposes by Annie E. K. Bidwell or Guy R. Kennedy, by deed or will, and such properties shall not be conveyed or exchanged.

The purchase or lease (whether as lessor or lessee) of real property shall be approved by the council, except as otherwise provided in this Charter.

Section 615: Same; Attesting

All ordinances and resolutions shall be attested to by the city clerk, but need not be signed by any other officer except as otherwise required by this Charter.

Section 616: Same; Effective Date

Except as otherwise herein provided to the contrary, ordinances shall become effective on the 30th day following date of adoption, provided that such ordinance has been published as provided by Section 611 within fifteen (15) days from date of adoption. In the event publication has not been so made, then such ordinance shall become effective on the 15th day following the date of publication. The following ordinances are expressly excepted from the foregoing requirements, and shall take effect upon adoption:

(A) An ordinance calling or otherwise relating to an election;

(B) An improvement proceeding ordinance adopted under some law or procedural ordinance;

(C) An emergency ordinance adopted in the manner provided for in this article.

Section 617: **Same; Codification and Adoption by Reference**

Ordinances establishing rules and regulations for the construction of buildings, including, but not limited to the installation of plumbing, electrical wiring, outdoor signs, or other similar work of construction or installation, and governing conditions hazardous to life and property, and a code of existing and properly adopted ordinances where such rules and regulations or ordinance codes have been printed as a code or codes in book form may be adopted by reference to such code or codes or such portions thereof in the manner provided by the general laws of the State of California. Ordinances of the City of Chico may adopt by reference as all or a part of such ordinance all or any portion of any general law of the State of California, without including the specific wording of such law in such ordinance.

Article VII: The City Manager

Section 700: Qualification

There shall be a city manager who shall be the chief administrator of the city. The city manager shall be appointed by the council and shall serve at its pleasure. The city manager shall not be removed from office except by the affirmative vote of at least four (4) members of the council. The city manager shall be chosen on the basis of executive and administrative qualifications. The city manager need not be a resident of the city or state at the time of appointment.

Section 701: Duties and Authority Generally

The city manager shall be the chief executive officer and the head of the administrative branch of the city government. The city manager shall be responsible to the council for the administration of all units of the city government under the city manager's jurisdiction and for carrying out policies adopted by the council. The city manager shall be charged with the preservation of the public peace, welfare, health, the safety of persons and property, the enforcement of law and the development and utilization of the city's resources.

The city manager shall:

(A) Appoint, discipline and remove, subject to the personnel system ordinance of the city, all officers and employees of the city except as otherwise provided by this Charter. The city manager may authorize the head of any department or office to appoint, discipline or remove subordinates in such department or office.

(B) Prepare the budget annually, submit it to the council, and be responsible for its administration after its adoption.

(C) Prepare and submit to the council as of the end of the fiscal year, a complete report on the finances, physical inventory and administrative activities of the city for the preceding year.

(D) Keep the council advised of the financial condition and future needs of the city and make such recommendations on any matter as may to the city manager seem desirable.

(E) Perform such other duties as may be prescribed by this Charter or required of the city manager by the council not inconsistent with this Charter.

The city manager may have the privilege to take part in the discussion of all matters coming before the council, but shall not vote.

Article VIII: Executive and Administrative Organizations

Section 800: Establishment by Ordinance

After obtaining and considering the recommendations of the city manager, the council shall provide by ordinance, not inconsistent with this Charter, for the organization, function, conduct and operation of the several offices, departments, and boards and commissions of the city, and may provide for the creation of additional departments, boards and commissions, divisions, offices and agencies, and for their consolidation, alteration, abolition, or reassignment.

Article IX: Appointive Officers and Employees

Section 900: Enumerated

The officers of the city shall consist of a city manager, city clerk, city attorney, city finance director, and such other officers as are required by law, or as the council may provide by ordinance.

Section 901: Residence Requirements

There shall be no residence requirements for any city officer or employee, except that by ordinance the city council may require that specific officers or employees reside within a reasonable and specified distance from their place of employment or other designated locations upon finding that such residence is reasonably related to performance of the officer's or employee's job.

Section 902: Oath of Office

Every officer, employee, department head and appointed official of the city, before entering upon the duties of the office for or to which such officer, employee or department head was employed, appointed or elected, shall take the oath of office as provided for in the Constitution of the State of California, and shall file the same with the city clerk.

Section 903: Official Bonds

The city council shall fix by ordinance or resolution the amounts and terms of the official bonds of all officials or employees who are required by law to give such bonds. All shall be executed by responsible corporate surety, shall be approved as to form by the city attorney, and shall be filed with the city clerk. Premiums on official bonds shall be paid by the city.

There shall be no personal liability upon, or any right to recover against, a superior officer, or such superior officer's bond, for any wrongful act or omission of such superior officer's subordinate, unless such superior officer was a part to, or conspired in, such wrongful act or omission.

Section 904: **Duties to be Established by Ordinance; Combining Departments or Offices; Suspending or Abolishing Offices**

The council shall provide by ordinance or resolution, not inconsistent with this Charter, for the powers and duties of all officers and department heads of the city. Where the positions are not incompatible, the council may combine in one person the powers and duties of two or more offices created or provided for in the Charter. When the city has contracted with the County of Butte for the assessment and collection of taxes, the council may suspend or abolish any office relating to the assessment or collection of taxes. No office provided herein to be filled by appointment by the city manager may be combined with an office provided herein to be filled by appointment of the council.

Section 905: **Powers and Duties of City Clerk**

The city clerk shall:

(A) Attend meetings of the council and be responsible for the recording and maintaining of a full and true record of all proceedings of the council in books that shall bear appropriate title and be devoted to such purpose; call the roll of the council and record the council members present, absent or excused.

(B) Maintain books in which shall be recorded respectively all duly adopted ordinances and resolutions, and, as to an ordinance requiring publication, an affidavit of publication or posting shall be affixed thereto.

(C) Maintain books in which a record shall be made of all written contracts and official bonds.

(D) Keep all aforementioned books properly indexed.

(E) Be the custodian of the seal of the city.

(F) Administer oaths or affirmations, taking affidavits and depositions pertaining to the affairs and business of the city and certify copies of the official records.

(G) Have charge of all elections to be conducted by the city, provided, that the city may contract with the County of Butte or any public officer authorized to conduct elections for the performance of all duties of conducting such elections.

(H) Perform such other duties consistent with this Charter as may be required by the council or by law.

Section 906:   Qualifications, Powers and Duties of City Attorney

The city attorney shall be an attorney at law, duly admitted to practice by the Supreme Court of the State of California, and licensed by said state to practice therein, and shall have been engaged in the practice of law in the state for a period of not less than five (5) years immediately prior to appointment. The city attorney shall:

(A) Represent and advise the city council, city officers, boards and commissions in all matters of law pertaining to their offices.

(B) Represent and appear for the city in any or all actions or proceedings in which the city is concerned or is a party, and represent and appear for any city officer, employee, board or commission, or former city officer, employee, board or commission, in any or all actions and proceedings in which any such officer, employee, board or commission is concerned or is a party arising out of any act or omission committed in the course and scope of the employment or performance of the official duties of such officer, employee, board or commission.

(C) Attend meetings of the city council and give advice or render an opinion in writing whenever requested to do so by the city council, or by any of the boards, commissions or officers of the city, provided that the city attorney may require such request to be submitted in writing.

(D) Approve the form of all contracts made by and all bonds given to the city, endorsing such contracts or bonds with such approval.

(E) Prepare or approve any and all proposed ordinances or resolutions for the city and amendments thereto.

(F) Appoint, discipline and remove any assistant city attorney, deputy city attorney or legal technician, provided that the appointment of a person by the city attorney to the position of assistant city attorney or deputy city attorney shall be subject to confirmation by the city council.

Section 906: Repealed

Section 907: Repealed

Section 908: **Finance Director**

The finance director shall be responsible for administration of the financial affairs of the city.

The finance director shall have custody of all public funds belonging to the city or to any office, department, board or commission or agency thereof, and shall administer all such funds in compliance with the provisions of the Constitution and laws of the State of California governing the collection, handling, depositing, investment and securing of public funds.

The finance director shall submit to the council through the city manager monthly statements of receipts, disbursements and balances in such form as to show the exact financial condition of the city. At the end of each fiscal year the finance director shall submit a complete and detailed financial statement.

Section 909: Compensation of Officers, Department Heads and Employees

The compensation of all city officers and department heads, except as otherwise provided in this Charter, shall be fixed by the council by resolution, and the compensation of all other city employees shall be determined in accordance with the personnel system ordinance. No officer, department head or employee shall be allowed any fees, perquisites, emoluments or compensation for the performance of the duties of the employment or office for or to which such officer, department head or employee was employed, appointed or elected, other than reimbursement for necessary expenses, and the compensation as determined in the manner herein provided.

Section 910: Repealed

Section 911: Nepotism

The council shall not appoint to a salaried position under the city government any person who is a relative by blood or marriage within the second degree of any one or more of the members of such council. Neither shall any board or commission, department head, or other officer having appointive power appoint any relative within such degree to any salaried position.

Section 912: **Delivery of Books, Papers, etc., to Successors**

All papers, books, documents, records, archives and other properties prepared for or purchased by the city shall be and remain the property of the city.

All officers, department heads, boards, commissions, and employees, upon leaving office, shall deliver to their successors all such papers, documents, records, books, archives and other such properties pertaining and belonging to their respective offices or department in their possession or under their control.

Section 913: **Inspection of Books and Records**

Except as otherwise provided by law, all books and records of every office and department shall be open to the inspection of any citizen during business hours, subject to the proper rules and regulations for the efficient conduct of the business of such department or office.

Section 914: **Copies from Books or Records**

Duly certified copies of records open for inspection shall be provided by the officer, department head or employee having the same in custody to any person demanding the same and paying the fee, if any, set by resolution of the council.

Article X: Appointive Boards and Commissions

Section 1000: Generally

There shall exist within the city each of the boards and commissions provided for by this article and any other board or commission now or hereafter established by ordinance of the council. Each such board and commission shall have the powers and duties provided for in this Charter and/or established by ordinance or resolution of the council; provided, however, that no power granted to a board or commission herein shall be deemed to be equal to or greater than that of the council.

Section 1000.1: Number of Members

The number of members comprising any board or commission shall be determined by ordinance of the council; provided, however, that no board or commission shall consist of less than five members.

Section 1001: Appointments; Terms

(A) Members of each board or commission shall be appointed by the council. In order to be eligible for an appointment to any board or commission, persons shall be residents of the city and qualified voters as defined by the Elections Code of the State of California.

(B) Members of each board or commission shall be appointed to serve a term of four (4) years and until their respective successors are appointed and qualified. The ordinance determining the number of members to comprise any board or commission shall provide that the four-year terms of members shall be staggered so that a substantially equal number of members shall have their terms commence at 7:30 p.m. on January 1st of every second year, except with respect to commissions having more than seven (7) members, who shall have their terms staggered so that a substantially equal number of the members thereof shall have their terms commence at 7:30 p.m. on January 1st of each year.

(C) A member of any board or commission may be removed from office at any time at the discretion of the council by an action of the council adopted by at least four (4) affirmative votes.

Section 1002: Repealed

Section 1003: **Organization**

(A) Each board or commission shall, at the first regular meeting of each calendar year, organize by electing one of its members to serve as presiding officer at the pleasure of such board or commission.

(B) Each board or commission shall hold regular meetings as required by ordinance of the council, and such special meetings as each board or commission may require. Written notice of such special meeting and the purpose thereof must be given not less than twenty-four (24) hours before the meeting to each member of the board or commission calling such special meeting, or within that time prescribed by state law, whichever is greater. All meetings and proceedings shall be open to the public, except as otherwise provided by law. Each board or commission shall keep a record of its proceedings and transactions, and a copy thereof shall be filed monthly with the city manager.

Section 1004: **Compensation**

Members of boards and commissions shall serve without compensation for their services, as such, but may be reimbursed for necessary travel and other expenses incurred on official duty when such expenditures have been budgeted or otherwise authorized by the council.

Section 1005: **Vacancies**

Vacancies in any board or commission, from whatever cause arising, shall be filled by appointment by the council for the unexpired portion of the term of the vacant office. If a member of a board or commission is convicted of a crime involving moral turpitude or ceases to be an elector of the city, the member's office shall become vacant and shall be so declared by the council.

Section 1006: **Bidwell Park and Playground Commission; Creation and Appointment of Members; Suspension**

The council shall appoint a board of park commissioners to be known as the Bidwell Park and Playground commission except during such time as the council shall, by resolution or ordinance, have determined that the conditions for suspension of the Bidwell Park and Playground commission exist, as hereinafter provided in subsection 1 of this section, which condition of suspension so determined shall have the effects set out in subsection 2 herein:

(1) Conditions of Suspension. The conditions of suspension referred to in this section are as follows:

- **(A)** Bidwell Park, Children's Playground and such other city parks and playgrounds as the city council deems appropriate are leased to another public entity.

- **(B)** The territory of said public entity includes entirely within its boundaries the territory within the city limits of the city of Chico.

(C) The terms of the agreement pursuant to which said properties are leased requires the lessee public entity to operate, maintain, and improve said properties for the benefit of the citizens and residents of the city of Chico, and may provide for the use of said properties by residents and citizens of the territory of the public entity, as well as others who may not be practically excluded.

(D) The lease agreement referred to above shall provide that the level of uses and benefit of said properties by citizens and residents of the city shall not be significantly curtailed or altered without consent of the council.

(E) The agreement referred to herein need not be specifically denoted a lease agreement so long as the effect is the same, and provided further that nothing herein authorizes the sale or conveyance of title to any of said park or playground properties to any public entity.

(2) Determination and Effect of Suspension. At any time that the conditions for suspension set out in subdivision 1 herein exist, the council may by resolution or ordinance find and determine such existence and order that a state of suspension exists. In the same manner, the council may rescind such resolution or ordinance by finding and determining that the conditions for suspension do not exist, provided, however, that they shall, at the same time, appoint a board of park commissioners as provided in the initial provision of this section. Upon an order that a state of suspension exists the following shall occur:

(A) All powers and duties conferred upon the Bidwell Park and Playground commission in this Charter or in the ordinances of the city of Chico shall cease and the terms of the members of such commission shall be forthwith terminated.

(B) The council shall be responsible for the propagation, planting, removing, pruning, and maintenance of all trees and shrubberies on the streets and along the sidewalks of the city. The council shall adopt such ordinances as may be necessary to exercise such responsibilities and may in such ordinances delegate the responsibility to any other board, commission or department of the city as it determines.

(C) The council shall accept the donations, legacies or bequests referred to in Section 1006.2 of this Charter.

(D) The council shall perform or provide by ordinance for the performance of all other responsibilities of the Bidwell Park and Playground commission regardless of the source of the imposition of such responsibility.

Upon a determination by the council that the conditions for suspension do not exist, the provisions of this subsection 2 shall cease to apply and the powers, duties and responsibilities of the Bidwell Park and Playground commission shall again exist as though no suspension had occurred.

Section 1006.1:   Same; Powers and Duties

The Bidwell Park and Playground commission, except when suspended as provided in this Charter, shall have the following powers and duties:

(A) The power and duty to operate and maintain all of the parks and playgrounds owned by the city and to adopt such rules and regulations as may be necessary to govern and control the use of such parks and playgrounds.

(B) The power and duty to provide for the propagation, planting, removing, pruning and maintenance of all trees and shrubberies along the streets and sidewalks of the city and to adopt such rules and regulations as may be necessary to govern and control the planting, removal, pruning, and maintenance of such trees and shrubberies.

(C) The power to enter into leases and contracts in connection with the operation of the properties under its supervision; provided, however, that any lease in excess of 15 years or any contract which encumbers city funds shall first require prior approval of the council; and, provided further, that no power granted herein shall be deemed to confer upon the Bidwell Park and Playground commission the right to sell or convey title to any city property.

(D) The power to confirm the appointment of the park director by the city manager, as hereinbefore provided in this Charter.

Section 1006.2: Same; Acceptance and Disposition of Donations, Legacies or Bequests

In the name of the city, except when suspended as provided in this Charter, the Bidwell Park and Playground commission may accept donations, legacies or bequests for the aid and improvement of the parks and playgrounds under its supervision, provided that all moneys derived from such donations, legacies or bequests shall, unless otherwise provided under the terms of such donations, legacies or bequests, be deposited in the treasury of the city to be used for the aid and improvement of the parks and playgrounds of the city subject to the terms of such donations, legacies or bequests.

Section 1007: **Airport Commission; Generally; Appointment of Members**

The council shall appoint a board of airport commissioners to be known as the airport commission.

Section 1007.1: **Same; Powers and Duties**

The airport commission shall have the following powers and duties:

(A) The power and duty to operate and maintain all airports and airport properties belonging to or under the control of the city and to adopt such rules and regulations as may be necessary to govern the use of such airports and airport properties.

(B) The power to enter into leases and contracts in connection with the operation of all airports and airport properties belonging to or under the control of the city; provided, however, that any lease in excess of 15 years or any contract which encumbers city funds shall first require prior approval of the council; and, provided further, that no power granted herein shall be deemed to confer upon the airport commission the right to sell or convey title to any city property.

(C) The power to confirm the appointment of the airport manager made by the city manager as hereinbefore provided in this Charter.

Section 1008: Repealed

Section 1008.1: Repealed

Section 1008.2: Repealed

Section 1008.3: Repealed

Section 1008.4: Repealed

Section 1009: Repealed

Section 1009.1: Repealed

Article XI: Fiscal Administration

Section 1100: The Fiscal Year

Unless otherwise provided by ordinance, the fiscal year of the City of Chico shall begin on the first day of July of each year and end on the 30th day of June the following year.

Section 1101: Tax System

The council may, by ordinance, provide a system for assessment and for the levy and collection of city taxes upon real and personal property.

Section 1102: Annual or Biennial Budget

The city manager shall prepare and present to the council a proposed budget for the ensuing fiscal year on or before the first day of the month preceding the commencement of such fiscal year. However, if the council elects to prepare a biennial budget pursuant to Section 1103, the city manager shall prepare and present to the council a proposed biennial budget for the next two succeeding fiscal years on or before the first day of the month preceding commencement of the first fiscal year addressed in such budget. The city manager shall append to each proposed budget the budget requests of those city departments, boards, and commissions for which special funds are established.

Section 1103: Budget; Adoption; Fixing of Tax Rates and Assessments

(A) The council shall consider and adopt by resolution a preliminary budget for the ensuing fiscal year during the month immediately preceding commencement of that fiscal year and shall adopt by resolution a final budget for that fiscal year at or before its first regular meeting held in such fiscal year.

(B) Notwithstanding subsection A, the council may, in its sole discretion, elect to adopt a biennial budget for the next two (2) succeeding fiscal years in lieu of annual budgets for such fiscal years. Such election shall be made by resolution of the council adopted before the first day of January preceding commencement of the first fiscal year to be addressed by a biennial budget. Thereafter, the council shall consider and adopt by resolution a preliminary biennial budget during the month immediately preceding commencement of the first fiscal year of the biennial period to be addressed by such budget, and adopt by resolution a final biennial budget at or before its first regular meeting held in the first fiscal year of the biennial period addressed by such budget.

The council shall continue to consider and adopt biennial budgets unless and until the council, by resolution adopted before the first day of January preceding a fiscal year, elects to return to the preparation and adoption of an annual budget, commencing with the next fiscal year.

(C) When adopting a final annual or biennial budget, the council may establish any tax rates or assessments as to taxes or assessments authorized by law to be included on the County of Butte property tax roll and collected simultaneously with property taxes.

Section 1104: **Funds**

There are hereby created the general, park, and airport funds and such other funds as may be established by the city council. All monies accruing to such funds shall be used only for the purposes for which such funds are established.

Section 1105: Repealed

Section 1106: **Special Taxes**

Whenever the council determines that the public interest demands an expenditure for municipal purposes which cannot be provided for out of the ordinary revenues of the city, it may submit to the qualified voters at a regular or special election, a proposition to provide for such expenditure, by levying a special tax, but no such special tax shall be levied unless authorized by the affirmative vote of the electors voting at such an election or as provided by the Constitution of the State of California.

Section 1107: **Revenue Bonds**

The council shall have the power to cause to be issued revenue bonds for the purpose of financing the acquisition, construction or reconstruction of public or publicly owned improvements of an income-producing character, either pursuant to the provisions of a procedural ordinance duly and regularly adopted by the council, or pursuant to the provisions of any general law of the State of California. If a procedural ordinance is adopted by the city it may, by reference, include therein any or all of the provisions of any one or more General Law Revenue Bond Acts or Assessment District Acts of the State of California.

Section 1108: **Limitation on Bonded Indebtedness**

The city shall not incur an indebtedness evidenced by general obligation bonds which shall in the aggregate exceed fifteen (15) percent of the total assessed valuation, for purpose of city taxation, of all the real and personal property within the city.

Section 1109: **Independent Audit**

At the beginning of each fiscal year, the council shall engage an independent certified public accountant, or public accountant licensed by the State Board of Accountancy, to act as auditor for the city, such engagement to be at the pleasure of the council. The auditor shall perform an annual audit of the books, financial records and related documents of the city in accordance with generally accepted auditing standards. On or prior to the first regular city council meeting in February of each year, unless an extension is granted by the council, the auditor shall submit to the council a report on the audit for the preceding fiscal year in such detail as the council may direct.

In addition to the regular annual audit, the auditor shall perform such other professional services as the council may require.

Section 1110: **Public Works Contracts**

City contracts which provide for the construction of a public works project, exclusive of maintenance and repair work, shall be competitively bid whenever the estimated cost of such public works project is equal to or exceeds the cost of a public works project required to be competitively bid under the general laws of the state of California applicable to public works contracts. Notice of intention to receive proposals shall be posted at least two weeks before the date of opening of the bids on the city's website, and it shall be posted in at least one public place in the city that has been designated for the posting of public notices; however, the council may designate a different method of notice by ordinance subject to the following conditions: (1) such ordinance shall provide for notice at least two weeks before the date of opening of the bids; and (2) such ordinance shall require notice to be posted in at least one public place in the city that has been designated for the posting of public notices. Such notice may give a description of the work to be done or may refer to plans and specifications on file in such office as may be specified in such notice. Should the bids received be deemed excessive or unsatisfactory, for any reason, or should no bids be received, the council, board or commission letting the contract may, by a majority vote of all its members, provide for the work to be done by the city manager.

Section 1111: **Form of Contract**

All contracts shall be in writing, approved by the city attorney, and executed in the name of the city by an officer or officers authorized to sign the same.

Section 1112: **Regulation of Public Works Contracts**

The formation, regulation and administration of contracts for public works is a municipal affair. This Charter and ordinances and resolutions adopted pursuant to it provide the basis of all contracts for or relating to public works to be designed, erected, constructed, installed, repaired, altered, improved, operated or maintained by the city. The general laws of the state shall not be deemed or construed to apply to any public works or contract for public works, including but not limited to the bidding or letting, terms and conditions, plans and specifications, or manner of administration of such contracts. However, the city may invoke, adopt, or incorporate by reference, in any ordinance, resolution, contract or plans and specifications for a public work, or relating to public works generally, all or part of any provision of the general laws of the state, including all or part of the Public Contract Code.

Section 1113: **Centralized Purchasing**

The city council shall adopt, by ordinance, policies and procedures governing centralized purchases of supplies and equipment for and by all city departments, boards, commissions, offices and agencies.

Section 1114: **Contracts for Legal Publications**

The council shall annually let contracts for publication of legal notices and official advertisements for the ensuing fiscal year. For this purpose the city clerk shall notify by mail each newspaper of general circulation in the city, as defined by California Government Code Section 6008, that sealed bids for such publications are to be received setting forth the details of the publications contemplated to be done. Each bidder shall include with its bid a verifiable statement of both net paid circulation and net unpaid circulation of its newspaper within the city. The council may accept more than one bid for these publications in any year and the city may then utilize one or more of these approved newspapers for any such publications.

In determining which bids are lowest and best, the council shall take into consideration the circulation, publication rates, and frequency of publication.

The council shall not accept any bid at a rate higher than that regularly charged by such bidding newspaper for the same or similar publications or advertising from other customers and may reject any and all bids.

The council may, if no acceptable bid is received, adopt any other legal method for legal publications.

If there is only one newspaper of general circulation in the City, the council may contract with it without advertising for bids.

Section 1115: **Claims, Demands, and Actions**

The city council shall adopt, by ordinance, procedures for the presentation of contract and tort claims for money or damages as prerequisite to suit against the city, its boards, commissions, agencies or departments and its elected officials as well as its officers, employees, or agents.

Article XII: Franchises

Section 1200: **Granting of Franchises**

Any person, firm or corporation furnishing the city or its inhabitants with any public utility or public service of any kind, or using the public streets, ways, alleys, or places for the operation of plants, works or equipment for the furnishing thereof, or traversing any portion of the city for any purpose, may be required by ordinance to have a valid and existing franchise therefor.

The council shall provide, by ordinance, the method of procedure and the terms and conditions under which such franchises may be granted. Such ordinance shall provide for public notice and public hearings. Any ordinance granting any franchise or privilege shall be published at the expense of the applicant therefor.

The council is empowered to grant such franchise by ordinance and to prescribe the terms and conditions of such grant. No franchise grant shall, in any way or to any extent, impair or affect the right of the city to acquire the property of the grantee thereof by eminent domain proceedings in the manner provided by law.

Article XIII:

Repealed

Article XIV: Personnel System

Section 1400: **Establishment by Ordinance**

Any officer authorized or empowered to appoint, employ, suspend or discharge, or fix the compensation of heads of departments, subordinate officials, officers, assistants, or employees of the city, shall exercise such authority or power subject to and in compliance with the provisions of any ordinance adopted by the city council establishing a personnel system.

Article XV: Miscellaneous

Section 1500: **Definitions**

Unless the provision or context otherwise requires, as used in this Charter:

(A) "Shall" is mandatory, and "may" is permissive;

(B) "City" is the City of Chico and "department," "board," "commission," "agency," "officer," or "employee," is a department, board, commission, agency, officer or employee, as the case may be, of the City of Chico;

(C) "County" is the County of Butte;

(D) "State" is the State of California;

(E) "Official newspaper of the city" is any newspaper which has been awarded a contract pursuant to Section 1114 of this Charter;

(F) The word "Council," wherever it occurs in this Charter, means the city council of the City of Chico.

Section 1501: **Powers Relative to Streams and Channels**

The city shall have power to improve the streams and channels within and without the city limits; to widen, straighten and deepen the channels thereof and remove obstructions therefrom; to construct and maintain embankments and other works to protect the city from overflow.

Section 1502: **Effective Date of Charter**

For the purpose of qualification and nomination of candidates for elective offices and the election of officers to fill offices created by this Charter, this Charter shall take effect from the time of its final approval by the state legislature. For all other purposes, it shall take effect on Tuesday, May 2, 1961, following approval by the legislature.

Section 1503: **Severability of Provisions of Charter**

If any section or part of a section of this Charter proves to be invalid, it shall not be held to invalidate or impair the validity of any other section or part of a section, unless it clearly appears that such other section or part of a section is dependent for its operation upon the section or part of a section so held invalid.

Section 1504: **Applicability of General Laws of State to City**

All general laws of the state applicable to municipal corporations, now or hereafter enacted, and which are not in conflict with the provisions of this Charter, or with ordinances or resolutions hereafter enacted, shall be applicable to the city.

Section 1505: **Violations; Penalties**

A violation of any provision of this Charter or of any ordinance or resolution of the city, or any order issued by any officer, agent or employee of the city pursuant to such ordinance or resolution shall be deemed an infraction unless such provision shall otherwise provide that such violation is a misdemeanor. All infractions shall be punished by a fine not exceeding one thousand dollars ($1,000.00) or as set by ordinance, and all misdemeanors shall be punished by a fine and/or imprisonment not exceeding the maximum penalty allowed under the general laws of the state for misdemeanors. A minimum penalty, not in excess of the maximum penalty provided for herein, may be adopted by ordinance with respect to any particular violation.

www.ingramcontent.com/pod-product-compliance
Lightning Source LLC
Chambersburg PA
CBHW071403210526
45465CB00001B/227